MASTER THE™ DSST®

Organizational
Behavior
Exam

About Peterson's

Peterson's® has been your trusted educational publisher for more than 50 years. It's a milestone we're quite proud of, as we continue to offer the most accurate, dependable, high-quality educational content in the field, providing you with everything you need to succeed. No matter where you are on your academic or professional path, you can rely on Peterson's for our books, online information, expert test-prep tools, the most up-to-date education exploration data, and the highest quality career success resources—everything you need to achieve your education goals. For our complete line of products, visit **www.petersons.com**.

For more information, contact Peterson's, 4380 S. Syracuse Street, Suite 200, Denver CO 80237; 800-338-3282 Ext. 54229; or visit us online at **www.petersons.com**.

ISBN-13: 978-0-7689-4465-5

Printed in the United States of America

10   9   8   7   6   5   4   3   2   1   24   23   22

Contents

Before You Begin

HOW THIS BOOK IS ORGANIZED

Peterson's *Master the*™ *DSST® Organizational Behavior Exam* provides a diagnostic test, subject-matter review, and a post-test.

- **Diagnostic Test**—Twenty multiple-choice questions, followed by an answer key with detailed answer explanations
- **Assessment Grid**—A chart designed to help you identify areas that you need to focus on based on your test results
- **Subject-Matter Review**—General overview of the exam subject, followed by a review of the relevant topics and terminology covered on the exam
- **Post-test**—Sixty multiple-choice questions, followed by an answer key and detailed answer explanations

The purpose of the diagnostic test is to help you figure out what you know—or don't know. The 20 multiple-choice questions are similar to the ones found on the DSST exam, and they should provide you with a good idea of what to expect. Once you take the diagnostic test, check your answers to see how you did. Included with each correct answer is a brief explanation regarding why a specific answer is correct, and in many cases, why other options are incorrect. Use the assessment grid to identify the questions you miss so that you can spend more time reviewing that information later. As with any exam, knowing your weak spots greatly improves your chances of success.

Following the diagnostic test is a subject-matter review. The review summarizes the various topics covered on the DSST exam. Key terms are defined; important concepts are explained; and when appropriate, examples are provided. As you read the review, some of the information may seem familiar while other information may seem foreign. Again, take note of the unfamiliar because that will most likely cause you problems on the actual exam.

After studying the subject-matter review, you should be ready for the post-test. The post-test contains sixty multiple-choice items, and it will serve as a dry run for the real DSST exam. There are complete answer explanations at the end of the test.

OTHER DSST® PRODUCTS BY PETERSON'S

Books, flashcards, practice tests, and videos available online at **www.petersons.com/testprep/dsst**

- A History of the Vietnam War
- Art of the Western World
- Astronomy
- Business Mathematics
- Business Ethics and Society
- Civil War and Reconstruction
- Computing and Information Technology
- Criminal Justice
- Environmental Science
- Ethics in America
- Ethics in Technology
- Foundations of Education
- Fundamentals of College Algebra
- Fundamentals of Counseling
- Fundamentals of Cybersecurity
- General Anthropology
- Health and Human Development
- History of the Soviet Union
- Human Resource Management

- Introduction to Business
- Introduction to Geography
- Introduction to Geology
- Introduction to Law Enforcement
- Introduction to World Religions
- Lifespan Developmental Psychology
- Math for Liberal Arts
- Management Information Systems
- Money and Banking
- Organizational Behavior
- Personal Finance
- Principles of Advanced English Composition
- Principles of Finance
- Principles of Public Speaking
- Principles of Statistics
- Principles of Supervision
- Substance Abuse
- Technical Writing

Like what you see? Get unlimited access to Peterson's full catalog of DSST practice tests, instructional videos, flashcards, and more at **www.petersons.com/testprep/dsst.**

Chapter 1

All About the DSST® Exam

WHAT IS DSST®?

Previously known as the DANTES Subject Standardized Tests, the DSST program provides the opportunity for individuals to earn college credit for what they have learned outside of the traditional classroom. Accepted or administered at more than 1,500 colleges and universities nationwide and approved by the American Council on Education (ACE), the DSST program enables individuals to use the knowledge they have acquired outside the classroom to accomplish their educational and professional goals.

WHY TAKE A DSST® EXAM?

DSST exams offer a way for you to save both time and money in your quest for a college education. Why enroll in a college course in a subject you already understand? For more than 30 years, the DSST program has offered the perfect solution for individuals who are knowledgeable in a specific subject and want to save both time and money. A passing score on a DSST exam provides physical evidence to universities of proficiency in a specific subject. More than 1,500 accredited and respected colleges and universities across the nation award undergraduate credit for passing scores on DSST exams. With the DSST program, individuals can shave months off the time it takes to earn a degree.

The DSST program offers numerous advantages for individuals in all stages of their educational development:

- Adult learners
- College students
- Military personnel

1

Adult learners desiring college degrees face unique circumstances—demanding work schedules, family responsibilities, and tight budgets. Yet adult learners also have years of valuable work experience that can frequently be applied toward a degree through the DSST program. For example, adult learners with on-the-job experience in business and management might be able to skip the Business 101 courses if they earn passing marks on DSST exams such as Introduction to Business and Principles of Supervision.

Adult learners can put their prior learning into action and move forward with more advanced course work. Adults who have never enrolled in a college course may feel a little uncertain about their abilities. If this describes your situation, then sign up for a DSST exam and see how you do. A passing score may be the boost you need to realize your dream of earning a degree. With family and work commitments, adult learners often feel they lack the time to attend college. The DSST program provides adult learners with the unique opportunity to work toward college degrees without the time constraints of semester-long course work. DSST exams take two hours or less to complete. In one weekend, you could earn credit for multiple college courses.

The DSST exams also benefit students who are already enrolled in a college or university. With college tuition costs on the rise, most students face financial challenges. The fee for each DSST exam starts at $100 (plus administration fees charged by some testing facilities)—significantly less than the $750 average cost of a 3-hour college class. Maximize tuition assistance by taking DSST exams for introductory or mandatory course work. Once you earn a passing score on a DSST exam, you are free to move on to higher-level course work in that subject matter, take desired electives, or focus on courses in a chosen major.

Not only do college students and adult learners profit from DSST exams, but military personnel reap the benefits as well. If you are a member of the armed services at home or abroad, you can initiate your post-military career by taking DSST exams in areas with which you have experience. Military personnel can gain credit anywhere in the world, thanks to the fact that almost all of the tests are available through the internet at designated testing locations. DSST testing facilities are located at more than 500 military installations, so service members on active duty can get a jump-start on a post-military career with the DSST program. As an additional incentive, DANTES (Defense Activity for Non-Traditional Education Support) provides funding for DSST test fees for eligible members of the military.

More than 30 subject-matter tests are available in the fields of Business, Humanities, Math, Physical Science, Social Sciences, and Technology.

Available DSST® Exams

Business	Social Sciences
Business Ethics and Society	A History of the Vietnam War
Business Mathematics	Art of the Western World
Computing and Information Technology	Criminal Justice
Human Resource Management	Foundations of Education
Introduction to Business	Fundamentals of Counseling
Management Information Systems	General Anthropology
Money and Banking	History of the Soviet Union
Organizational Behavior	Introduction to Geography
Personal Finance	Introduction to Law Enforcement
Principles of Finance	Lifespan Developmental Psychology
Principles of Supervision	Substance Abuse
	The Civil War and Reconstruction
Humanities	**Physical Sciences**
Ethics in America	Astronomy
Introduction to World Religions	Environmental Science
Principles of Advanced English	Health and Human Development
Composition	Introduction to Geology
Principles of Public Speaking	
Math	**Technology**
Fundamentals of College Algebra	Ethics in Technology
Math for Liberal Arts	Fundamentals of Cybersecurity
Principles of Statistics	Technical Writing

As you can see from the table, the DSST program covers a wide variety of subjects. However, it is important to ask two questions before registering for a DSST exam.

1. Which universities or colleges award credit for passing DSST exams?
2. Which DSST exams are the most relevant to my desired degree and my experience?

Knowing which universities offer DSST credit is important. In all likelihood, a college in your area awards credit for DSST exams, but find out before taking an exam by contacting the university directly. Then review the list of DSST exams to determine which ones are most relevant to the degree you are seeking and to your base of knowledge. Schedule an appointment with your college adviser to determine which exams best fit your degree program and which college courses the DSST exams can replace. Advisers should also be able to tell you the minimum score required on the DSST exam to receive university credit.

DSST® TEST CENTERS

You can find DSST testing locations in community colleges and universities across the country. Check the DSST website (**www.getcollegecredit. com**) for a location near you or contact your local college or university to find out if the school administers DSST exams. Keep in mind that some universities and colleges administer DSST exams only to enrolled students. DSST testing is available to men and women in the armed services at more than 500 military installations around the world.

HOW TO REGISTER FOR A DSST® EXAM

Once you have located a nearby DSST testing facility, you need to contact the testing center to find out the exam administration schedule. Many centers are set up to administer tests via the internet, while others use printed materials. Almost all DSST exams are available as online tests, but the method used depends on the testing center. The cost for each DSST exam starts at $100, and many testing locations charge a fee to cover their costs for administering the tests. Credit cards are the only accepted payment method for taking online DSST exams. Credit card, certified check, and money order are acceptable payment methods for paper-and-pencil tests.

Test takers are allotted two score reports—one mailed to them and another mailed to a designated college or university, if requested. Online tests generate unofficial scores at the end of the test session, while individuals taking paper tests must wait four to six weeks for score reports.

PREPARING FOR A DSST® EXAM

Even though you are knowledgeable in a certain subject matter, you should still prepare for the test to ensure you achieve the highest score possible. The first step in studying for a DSST exam is to find out what will be on the specific test you have chosen. Information regarding test content is located on the DSST fact sheets, which can be downloaded at no cost from **www.getcollegecredit.com**. Each fact sheet outlines the topics covered on a subject-matter test, as well as the approximate percentage assigned to each topic. For example, questions on the Organizational Behavior exam are distributed in the following way: Organizational Behavior Overview—10%, Individual Processes and Characteristics—30%, Interpersonal and Group Processes—30%, Organizational Processes and Characteristics—15%, and Change and Development Processes—15%.

In addition to the breakdown of topics on a DSST exam, the fact sheet also lists recommended reference materials. If you do not own the recommended books, then check college bookstores. Avoid paying high prices for new textbooks by looking online for used textbooks. Don't panic if you are unable to locate a specific textbook listed on the fact sheet; the textbooks are merely recommendations. Instead, search for comparable books used in university courses on the specific subject. Current editions are ideal, and it is a good idea to use at least two references when studying for a DSST exam. Of course, the subject matter provided in this book will be a sufficient review for most test takers. However, if you need additional information, then it is a good idea to have some of the reference materials at your disposal when preparing for a DSST exam.

Fact sheets include other useful information in addition to a list of reference materials and topics. Each fact sheet includes subject-specific sample questions like those you will encounter on the DSST exam. The sample questions provide an idea of the types of questions you can expect on the exam. Test questions are multiple-choice with one correct answer and three incorrect choices.

The fact sheet also includes information about the number of credit hours ACE has recommended be awarded by colleges for a passing DSST exam score. However, you should keep in mind that not all universities and colleges adhere to the ACE recommendation for DSST credit hours. Some institutions require DSST exam scores higher than the minimum score recommended by ACE. Once you have acquired appropriate reference materials and you have the outline provided on the fact sheet, you are ready to start studying, which is where this book can help.

TEST DAY

After reviewing the material and taking practice tests, you are finally ready to take your DSST exam. Follow these tips for a successful test day experience.

1. **Arrive on time.** Not only is it courteous to arrive on time to the DSST testing facility, but it also allows plenty of time for you to take care of check-in procedures and settle into your surroundings.

2. **Bring identification.** DSST test facilities require that candidates bring a valid government-issued identification card with a current photo and signature. Acceptable forms of identification include a current driver's license, passport, military identification card, or state-issued identification card. Individuals who fail to bring proper identification to the DSST testing facility will not be allowed to take an exam.

3. **Bring the right supplies.** If your exam requires the use of a calculator, you may bring a calculator that meets the specifications. For paper-based exams, you may also bring No. 2 pencils with an eraser and black ballpoint pens. Regardless of the exam methodology, you are NOT allowed to bring reference or study materials, scratch paper, or electronics such as cell phones, personal handheld devices, cameras, alarm wrist watches, or tape recorders to the testing center.

4. **Take the test.** During the exam, take the time to read each question-and-answer option carefully. Eliminate the choices you know are incorrect to narrow the number of potential answers. If a question completely stumps you, take an educated guess and move on—remember that DSSTs are timed; you will have 2 hours to take the exam.

With the proper preparation, DSST exams will save you both time and money. So join the thousands of people who have already reaped the benefits of DSST exams and move closer than ever to your college degree.

ORGANIZATIONAL BEHAVIOR EXAM FACTS

The DSST® Organizational Behavior exam consists of 100 multiple-choice questions designed to evaluate your knowledge in organizational behavior topics such as individual processes and characteristics, interpersonal and group processes, and change and development processes.

Area or Course Equivalent: Organizational Behavior
Level: Lower-level baccalaureate
Amount of Credit: 3 Semester Hours
Minimum Score: 400
Source: https://getcollegecredit.com/wp-content/uploads/2021/02/ ORG-BEHAVIOR.pdf

I. Organizational Behavior Overview – 10%

    a. The field of organizational behavior

        i. Definition and framework

        ii. Fundamental concepts

        iii. History

    b. The study of organizational behavior

        i. Scientific approaches

        ii. Research designs

        iii. Data collection methods

II. Individual Processes and Characteristics – 30%

    a. Perceptual processes

    b. Personality

    c. Attitudes and emotions

    d. Learning processes

    e. Motivation

    f. Work stress

III. Interpersonal and Group Processes – 30%

    a. Group dynamics

    b. Group behavior and conflict

    c. Leadership and influences

    d. Power and politics

    e. Communication processes

IV. Organizational Processes and Characteristics – 15%

    a. Organizational decision-making

    b. Organization structure and design

    c. Organization culture and strategy

V. Change and Development Processes – 15%

    a. Basic processes

    b. Concepts of change

    c. Applications and techniques of change and development

Chapter 2

Organizational Behavior Diagnostic Test

DIAGNOSTIC TEST ANSWER SHEET

1. Ⓐ Ⓑ Ⓒ Ⓓ	8. Ⓐ Ⓑ Ⓒ Ⓓ	15. Ⓐ Ⓑ Ⓒ Ⓓ
2. Ⓐ Ⓑ Ⓒ Ⓓ	9. Ⓐ Ⓑ Ⓒ Ⓓ	16. Ⓐ Ⓑ Ⓒ Ⓓ
3. Ⓐ Ⓑ Ⓒ Ⓓ	10. Ⓐ Ⓑ Ⓒ Ⓓ	17. Ⓐ Ⓑ Ⓒ Ⓓ
4. Ⓐ Ⓑ Ⓒ Ⓓ	11. Ⓐ Ⓑ Ⓒ Ⓓ	18. Ⓐ Ⓑ Ⓒ Ⓓ
5. Ⓐ Ⓑ Ⓒ Ⓓ	12. Ⓐ Ⓑ Ⓒ Ⓓ	19. Ⓐ Ⓑ Ⓒ Ⓓ
6. Ⓐ Ⓑ Ⓒ Ⓓ	13. Ⓐ Ⓑ Ⓒ Ⓓ	20. Ⓐ Ⓑ Ⓒ Ⓓ
7. Ⓐ Ⓑ Ⓒ Ⓓ	14. Ⓐ Ⓑ Ⓒ Ⓓ	

ORGANIZATIONAL BEHAVIOR DIAGNOSTIC TEST
24 minutes—20 questions

Directions: Carefully read each of the following 20 questions. Choose the best answer to each question and fill in the corresponding circle on the answer sheet. The Answer Key and Explanations can be found following this Diagnostic Test.

---

1. Jenna regularly attends gatherings at a local restaurant arranged by the professional marketing organization to which she belongs. She hopes to develop contacts with people outside her firm in case she ever needs to find a new job. Which of the following best describes Jenna's activities?

   A. Illegitimate political behavior
   B. Legitimate political behavior
   C. Integrative bargaining
   D. Risk aversion

2. Which of the following people first identified the ten roles of managers?

   A. Kurt Lewin
   B. Henri Fayol
   C. Henry Mintzberg
   D. Abraham Maslow

3. Which type of small-group network depends on a central figure to convey the group's communications?

   A. Single-channel
   B. All-channel
   C. Wheel
   D. Chain

4. The sales manager at Hoffman Car Dealership is concerned because of the dealership's low sales numbers over the last quarter. The sales manager blames the problem on the laziness of the sales team instead of on price incentives offered by competitors. Which of the following best explains the sales manager's beliefs?

A. Fundamental attribution error
B. Overconfidence bias
C. Self-serving bias
D. Contrast effect

5. Which of the following involves a sender purposely manipulating information so the receiver will view it favorably?

A. Selective perception
B. Monitoring
C. Dissemination
D. Filtering

6. Which employee personality trait has the most consistent correlation with organizational success?

A. Openness to new ideas
B. Conscientiousness
C. Agreeableness
D. Extraversion

7. Which of the following is NOT part of systematic study?

A. Observing relationships
B. Drawing conclusions based on evidence
C. Using intuition to come to conclusions
D. Identifying causes and effects

8. An employee states, "My pay is too low." Which attitude component is the employee most likely expressing?

A. Emotional
B. Cognition
C. Affect
D. Behavior

9. Which of the following are the three categories of primary causes of work stressors?

A. Environmental factors, organizational factors, and employee factors

B. Organizational factors, personal factors, and culture factors

C. Organizational factors, personal factors, and environmental factors

D. Employee factors, culture factors, and environmental factors

10. Which model of learning asserts that the consequences of actions shape voluntary behavior?

A. Observational learning

B. Classical conditioning

C. Situational learning

D. Operant conditioning

11. Which organizational design approach is most likely to generate confusion regarding authority?

A. Bureaucracy

B. Matrix

C. Simple

D. Product

12. Which of the following represents the highest level of Maslow's hierarchy of needs?

A. Achievement

B. Friendship

C. Security

D. Shelter

13. Which of the following is the decision-making model that assumes that decision makers have all available information, can identify relevant options, and can choose the most logical and sensible option?

A. Bounded rationality

B. Intuitive decision-making

C. Rational decision-making

D. Informed decision-making

14. What is one way to overcome resistance to organizational change?

    A. Provide employees with little information about the change
    B. Stimulate a culture of innovation
    C. Restricting group norms
    D. Asking employees to change their habits

15. Which of the following is NOT one of the causes of organization-wide resistance?

    A. Personal stressors
    B. Having to change habits
    C. Worrying about security
    D. Fear of the unknown

16. In the norming stage of group development, members are more likely to

    A. accomplish a specific task.
    B. establish a formal hierarchy.
    C. form close relationships.
    D. experience conflict.

17. Which term refers to making planned changes by improving the effectiveness of an organization through research, technology, and training?

    A. Effectiveness strategizing
    B. Organizational development
    C. Job design
    D. Organizational design

18. Which of the following statements best describes the transformational leadership theory?

    A. Leaders exhibit accuracy in decision-making.
    B. Leaders possess unique risk-taking behaviors.
    C. Leaders have specific personality traits.
    D. Leaders provide organizational vision.

19. Lewin's three-step model primarily addresses how organizations can

    A. minimize conflicts.
    B. implement changes.
    C. motivate workers.
    D. develop leaders.

20. A star quarterback has endorsement contracts with numerous firms, including an electronics manufacturer, a soft drink company, and a sports drink company. Advertisers are most likely hoping that the football star has

    A. referent power.
    B. coercive power.
    C. legitimate power.
    D. expert power.

ANSWER KEY AND EXPLANATIONS

1. B	5. D	9. C	13. C	17. B
2. C	6. B	10. D	14. B	18. D
3. C	7. C	11. B	15. A	19. B
4. A	8. B	12. A	16. C	20. A

1. **The correct answer is B.** Legitimate political behavior includes networking. Jenna is not involved in activities that would harm her employer, so choice A is incorrect. Choices C and D are irrelevant.

2. **The correct answer is C.** Henry Mintzberg is an academic who conducted research on management roles and identified ten of them. Kurt Lewin (choice A) developed an organizational change model. Henri Fayol (choice B) identified six functions of management and fourteen principles of management. Abraham Maslow (choice D) developed the theory of a hierarchy of needs.

3. **The correct answer is C.** A wheel network depends on one leader to relay information. A single-channel network (choice A) is not a type of small-group network. In an all-channel network (choice B), all members communicate with one another. Chain networks (choice D) follow hierarchies for communication.

4. **The correct answer is A.** Fundamental attribution error is the tendency to underestimate the power of external factors and overestimate the power of internal factors. Overconfidence bias (choice B) involves being too optimistic. A self-serving bias (choice C) involves attributing failures to external factors. Contrast effect (choice D) involves making comparisons between people, not blaming them.

5. **The correct answer is D.** Filtering occurs when a sender manipulates information. Selective perception (choice A) involves hearing what you want to hear. Monitoring (choice B) is not a type of communication barrier. Dissemination (choice C) involves sharing information, but not necessarily manipulating it.

6. The correct answer is B. The most important and consistent trait for both individual and organizational success is conscientiousness. Openness (choice A), agreeableness (choice C), and extraversion (choice D) are not as strongly related to organizational success.

7. The correct answer is C. Systematic study involves using the best scientific evidence, not intuition, to inform managerial decisions. This means research should involve observing relationships (choice A), drawing conclusions based on evidence (choice B), and identifying causes and effects (choice D).

8. The correct answer is B. Attitudes develop from three components: cognition, affect, and behavior. The cognitive component is an opinion, such as "My pay is too low." Emotions and feelings (choice A) are the affective component (choice C). The behavioral component (choice D) is the individual's intention to behave.

9. The correct answer is C. The primary causes of work stressors are categorized as organizational, personal, and environmental factors. Choice C is the only option that contains all three of these categories. Choices A, B, and D include other concepts that are not primary categories of work stressors.

10. The correct answer is D. The operant conditioning model made famous by B.F. Skinner linked behavior with consequences. Observational learning (choice A) asserts that people learn by imitating behaviors observed in other people. Classical conditioning (choice B) is incorrect because Pavlov linked associations with responses. Situational learning (choice C) is not a model of learning.

11. The correct answer is B. The matrix structure is more likely to cause employees confusion because of its dual line of command. Chain of command is clear in a bureaucracy (choice A) and in simple structures (choice C). Departments organized by product (choice D) are not likely to trigger leadership confusion.

12. **The correct answer is A.** Achievement falls in the category of ego, which is near the top of Maslow's hierarchy of needs. Friendship (choice B), security (choice C), and shelter (choice D) are lower than achievement on Maslow's hierarchy.

13. **The correct answer is C.** Rational decision-making relies on logic and objective analysis. Bounded rationality (choice A) accounts for some of the assumptions that aren't visible in the real world and assumes that decision makers search for solutions that are sufficient rather than ideal. Intuitive decision-making (choice B) involves making a decision based on a hunch. Choice D is not one of the decision-making models.

14. **The correct answer is B.** Stimulating a culture of innovation encourages creative, out-of-the-box ideas, involving employees in change. Providing employees with little information about organizational change (choice A), restricting group norms (choice C), and asking employees to change their habits (choice D) can all increase resistance to organizational change by posing threats to individuals.

15. **The correct answer is A.** Personal stressors, such as having to change habits, worrying about security, and fearing economic changes and the unknown, are common sources of an individual's resistance to organizational change. Since personal stressors are different for each individual, they aren't considered a cause of organization-wide resistance.

16. **The correct answer is C.** During the norming stage, members form close relationships and develop common expectations of member behavior. Accomplishing a specific task (choice A) occurs in the performing stage. Choices B and D are incorrect because a hierarchy forms and conflict occurs during the storming stage.

17. **The correct answer is B.** Organizational development refers to making planned changes by improving the effectiveness of an organization through research, technology, and training. Effectiveness strategizing (choice A) is not an organizational behavior term. Job design (choice C) refers to how an employee's job is structured. Organizational design (choice D) refers to the way in which the organization is structured.

18. **The correct answer is D.** The transformational leadership theory asserts that leaders convey visionary goals to followers. Choices A and B are not necessarily linked to the transformational leadership theory. Trait theories (choice C) focus on personal qualities.

19. **The correct answer is B.** Lewin's model describes the process of implementing organizational changes. Conflicts (choice A), motivation (choice C), and leadership (choice D) are not addressed.

20. **The correct answer is A.** Referent power stems from identifying with a person who has desirable personality traits and resources. Coercive power (choice B) relies on the fear of negative results. Legitimate power (choice C) refers to the formal authority to control. Choice D is not the best answer because although the star quarterback is a football expert, he is not necessarily an expert on electronics or soda.

DIAGNOSTIC TEST ASSESSMENT GRID

Now that you've completed the diagnostic test and read through the answer explanations, you can use your results to target your studying. Find the question numbers from the diagnostic test that you answered incorrectly and highlight or circle them below. Then focus extra attention on the sections dealing with those topics.

Organizational Behavior		
Content Area	**Topic**	**Question #**
Organizational Behavior Overview	• The field of organizational behavior • The study of organizational behavior	2, 7
Individual Processes and Characteristics	• Perceptual processes • Personality • Attitudes and emotions • Learning processes • Motivation • Work stress	4, 6, 8, 9, 10, 12
Interpersonal and Group Processes	• Group dynamics • Group behavior and conflict • Leadership and influences • Power and politics • Communication processes	1, 3, 5, 16, 18, 20
Organizational Processes and Characteristics	• Organizational decision-making • Organization structure and design • Organization culture and strategy	11, 13, 14
Change and Development Processes	• Basic processes • Concepts of change • Applications and techniques of change and development	15, 17, 19

Chapter 3

Organizational Behavior Subject Review

OVERVIEW

- The Field of Organizational Behavior
- The Study of Organizational Behavior
- Individual Processes and Characteristics
- Interpersonal and Group Processes
- Organizational Processes and Characteristics
- Change and Development Processes
- Summing It Up

Historically, business schools and corporations have focused on developing managers with effective technical skills and have given very little attention to improving the manager's interpersonal skills. However, modern businesses are realizing that managers need people skills on a daily basis to retain high-performing workers, handle employee conflicts, improve workplace productivity, and enhance both worker and firm performance. Organizational behavior addresses these essential managerial skills.

THE FIELD OF ORGANIZATIONAL BEHAVIOR

Organizational behavior is a field of study that emerged during the 1980s as businesses began to realize the connection between organizational performance and employee behavior. It involves analyzing the effect that individuals, groups, and structure have on an organization's performance.

NOTE: Ten percent of the questions on your DSST exam will cover general questions about organizational behavior.

While the field of organizational behavior only developed within the last three or four decades, the study of management began much earlier. Henri Fayol, an early twentieth-century French businessman, developed the first theory of management. According to Fayol, professional management involved the functions of planning, organizing, commanding, coordinating, and controlling. **Fayolism** has since been condensed to planning, organizing, leading, and controlling.

In the 1960s, Canadian academic Henry Mintzberg studied five executives for two weeks to determine what they did as managers. Mintzberg identified ten roles that can be categorized as interpersonal, informational, or decisional. It's important to note that the roles and their associated behaviors are highly interconnected.

Mintzberg's Management Roles	
Interpersonal	• *Figurehead:* performs routine duties as symbolic leader • *Leader:* motivates and directs workers • *Liaison:* maintains a network of outside contacts
Informational	• *Monitor:* receives information • *Disseminator:* transmits information to organization members • *Spokesperson:* transmits information to outsiders
Decisional	• *Entrepreneur:* initiates projects and searches for opportunities • *Disturbance Handler:* takes corrective action when problems occur • *Resource Allocator:* makes or approves organizational decisions • *Negotiator:* represents the organization at significant negotiations

The historical underlying purpose of studying managers has been to improve the performance and effectiveness of an organization. Hence, it was a natural progression that led to the field of organizational behavior. By understanding the impact that individuals, groups, and structures have on organizational performance, firms can function more effectively.

THE STUDY OF ORGANIZATIONAL BEHAVIOR

Although organizational behavior benefits numerous settings, it is primarily intended to help managers handle workplace situations such as employee motivation, absenteeism, turnover, and productivity. The following table provides an overview of core topics studied at each level of an organization.

Types of Organizational Behavior	
Individual	Perceptual processes, personality, attitudes, learning processes, motivation, and work stress
Group	Dynamics, conflict, leadership, power, politics, and communication processes
Structure	Decision-making processes, organizational structure, organizational design, and change processes

Although some managers may have a knack for "reading" people, such attempts at predicting or interpreting behavior often lead to false assumptions. Managers improve their chances of making accurate predictions by balancing personal intuition with research derived from systematic study.

Systematic study involves observing relationships, identifying causes and effects, and drawing conclusions based on evidence. The most commonly used research design methods are:

- Case studies
- Field surveys
- Laboratory experiments
- Field experiments
- Aggregate quantitative reviews

Psychology, social psychology, sociology, and anthropology are the fields of study that provide the primary research contributions. Evidence-based management is a growing trend resulting from the vast body of research now available. Rather than relying on hunches and intuition, adherents of evidence-based management rely on the best scientific evidence to make managerial decisions.

INDIVIDUAL PROCESSES AND CHARACTERISTICS

Because individual employees have a significant impact on an organization's performance, understanding individual processes is important in the field of organizational behavior. Perceptions, personalities, attitudes, learning processes, motivations, and stress factors will be discussed in the following sections.

NOTE: A high number of questions (30 percent) on your DSST exam will test your knowledge of individual processes and characteristics.

Perceptual Processes

Behavior is based on individual perceptions of the world, so understanding perceptual processes is essential in the study of organizational behavior. **Perceptions** are how individuals organize and interpret what they experience, which may differ significantly from reality. In the workplace, for example, one employee may perceive a firm's benefits package as exceptional, while another employee may perceive the same compensation as mediocre. In another situation, one coworker may be perceived as loud and obnoxious by some but perceived as a leader by other individuals.

Three key factors explain why employees frequently have such different perceptions:

1. The perceiver
2. The target
3. The situation

An individual perceiver's attitudes, motives, interests, experiences, and expectations influence personal perceptions. The target or object being perceived has certain distinguishing characteristics that influence perceptions either positively or negatively. For example, a young worker may be perceived as having poor work habits, while a defense attorney may be perceived as unethical. The situation or context also plays a role in perception. A female employee who wears a short skirt to work may be viewed as unprofessional, but if she wears the same skirt to a party, the perceptions would most likely change.

Although perceptions may seem to occur automatically, people are actually employing various techniques when making judgments. These techniques are useful because they speed up the perception process, but they may also act as barriers to accurate perceptions. Understanding the methods and their associated problems will enhance the accuracy of the perception process.

Methods of Perception		
Method	Description	Problem
Selective Perception	Interpreting only selected observations of a person based on personal interests, experiences, and attitudes	Quick, narrow interpretations lead to unfounded conclusions
Halo Effect	Drawing general impressions of a person based on one characteristic	Single traits influence broad conclusions.
Contrast Effects	Evaluating a person's characteristics by making comparisons to another person	Misperceptions occur because individuals are not evaluated in isolation.
Stereotyping	Judging a person based on group association	Generalizations are often unfair and untrue.

The perceptions people develop about one another are known as **person perceptions**. Scientists have attempted to explain the different ways that judgments are made through attribution theory. According to **attribution theory**, people try to explain the behavior of others based on internal or external attributes. Behaviors that occur because of internal attributes are under the control of an individual, whereas externally caused behaviors are out of the individual's control. For example, a manager who attributes an employee's tardiness to laziness is making an internal attribution. If the manager attributes the employee's tardiness to bad traffic, she is making an external attribution. Determining whether a person's behavior is caused by internal or external factors depends on the following factors:

- **Distinctiveness:** Does the person behave differently in different situations? If the late employee also fails to complete tasks on time, then the behavior would be judged as an internal attribute. However, if the employee typically performs well, then an external attribution would most likely be made.
- **Consensus:** Does everyone behave similarly when faced with a similar situation? If numerous employees are also late, then the behavior shows consensus and would be attributed to external causes.
- **Consistency:** Does the person behave similarly over a period of time? If the late employee is regularly late, then the behavior would most likely be internally attributed.

Research shows that attributions are often distorted by fundamental attribution errors and self-serving biases. The fundamental attribution error is the tendency to place more value on internal factors than external ones. The tendency of individuals to attribute successes to internal causes and failures to external causes is known as a **self-serving bias**.

Personality

In the field of organizational behavior, **personality** refers to an individual's pattern of reactions in terms of behavior, thoughts, and actions that tend to remain stable over time and across situations. Research indicates that personality traits are determined by a combination of genetic and environmental factors. Characteristics that an individual exhibits in many situations are considered personality traits. Two primary tools are used to identify and classify personality traits: the **Myers-Briggs Type Indicator (MBTI)** and the **Big Five model**.

NOTE: Recent trends in research are focusing on evaluating other personality traits that could have an influence on individual and organizational outcomes. Such findings are early, but some of these traits are proactivity, adaptability, and emotional intelligence. Since research on these traits is still new, the MBTI and Big Five model are still the main tools for assessing personality in organizational behavior research.

The MBTI, which consists of 100 questions, is the most frequently used personality-assessment tool. Individuals are identified as one of sixteen personality types identified by a four-letter combination. The MBTI test results determine which four of the following eight characteristics best describes a person:

1. **Extraverted or Introverted:** Extraverts are outgoing and sociable, while introverts are quiet and shy.
2. **Sensing or Intuitive:** Sensing individuals are practical and detail-oriented, whereas intuitive individuals focus on future possibilities.
3. **Thinking or Feeling:** Thinking individuals solve problems with logic, whereas feeling individuals depend on emotions.
4. **Judging or Perceiving:** Judging individuals prefer control in an orderly world, whereas perceiving individuals are adaptable and spontaneous.

The MBTI is used by many large organizations, and it serves as a useful tool for career guidance. However, the MBTI is based on questionable evidence and is not recommended as a selection assessment.

In contrast, the Big Five model is supported by a large body of evidence regarding the tool's five personality traits:

1. **Extraversion:** comfort level with relations
2. **Agreeableness:** tendency to defer to others
3. **Conscientiousness:** measure of reliability
4. **Emotional stability:** ability to handle stress
5. **Openness to experience:** range of interests and creativity

Studies have indicated a strong connection between the personality dimensions of the Big Five model and job performance. The most important and consistent trait for both individual and organizational success is conscientiousness. The following table indicates the link between high scores in each of the five traits and any positive or negative work behaviors.

Influence of Big Five Traits on Job Performance	
Trait	Significance
Extraversion	• Higher job satisfaction, better interpersonal skills, and higher job performance • More impulsive and more likely to be absent and partake in risky behaviors
Agreeableness	• More compliant, better likeability, and higher job performance • Lower levels of career success and negotiation skills
Conscientiousness	• Better organization, better attention to detail, more persistence, and higher job performance • Lower ability to adapt to change and think creatively
Emotional Stability	• Lower stress levels, higher job satisfaction, and less negative thinking
Openness	• More adaptable to change, more creative, and enhanced leadership • More susceptible to workplace accidents

Attitudes and Emotions

In the field of organizational behavior, positive or negative evaluations of objects, people, or events are referred to as **attitudes**. Attitudes develop from three components:

1. Cognition
2. Affect
3. Behavior

The **cognitive** component is an opinion, such as, "My boss is unfair." The **affective** and **emotional** component is a feeling, such as, "I'm angry about how much work I have to do on the weekend." The **behavioral** component is the individual's intention to behave, such as, "I'm going to look for a better job that requires less overtime."

Attitudes are typically connected to **values**, which are the convictions that a person has about what is right, wrong, or desirable. Values serve as the basis for understanding people's attitudes and motivations. The **Rokeach Value Survey**, developed by the social psychologist Milton Rokeach, presents a philosophical basis for the association of values with beliefs and attitudes. According to the Rokeach Value Survey, values can be divided into two types: terminal values and instrumental values. **Terminal values** are goals that an individual would like to accomplish during a lifetime, such as prosperity, equality, family security, happiness, and wisdom. **Instrumental values** are the means to achieving terminal values, and they are exhibited through behaviors such as hard work, truthfulness, sincerity, dependability, and honesty. Studies indicate that individuals holding similar positions have similar values and vice versa. Such information is important in organizations, as conflicts may arise because executives and hourly workers, for example, have different values.

Research shows that several factors influence job attitudes: job characteristics, emotions, the social environment, leadership, and organizational policies and practices. Job attitudes are such a large area of research within organizational behavior because they have the ability to impact a variety of outcomes including job performance, creativity, withdrawal behaviors, counterproductive work, extra-role helping behaviors, and organizational performance.

Although everyone holds many different attitudes, organizational behaviorists primarily focus on the following key employee attitudes.

Key Employee Attitudes	
Job satisfaction	Positive or negative feelings about a job based on evaluations of the job's characteristics
Job involvement	The extent to which employees identify and care about their job
Organizational commitment	The extent to which employees identify with the goals of an organization and want to continue as members
Perceived organizational support	The extent to which employees believe an organization cares for their well-being and values their work
Employee engagement	An employee's job-related involvement, satisfaction, and enthusiasm

Managers benefit from a strong understanding of employee attitudes, because satisfied and committed workers are more productive and less likely to quit.

While employee attitudes tend to be more stable over time, affect and emotion are shorter in duration and are triggered by specific events or stimuli. According to the **Circumplex Model of Affect**, emotions can be defined according to where they fall on two dimensions: energy (from low to high) and pleasantness (from low to high). For example, an emotion with high energy and low pleasantness is nervousness. An emotion with low negative affectivity and low energy would be calmness.

Emotions are important because positive emotions tend to be associated with better outcomes for individuals and organizations (e.g., improved work performance, better supervisor evaluations, effective decision-making, creativity, and fewer intentions to leave the organization). Research also shows that emotions are contagious and can be transferred from one person to the rest of a work group. Therefore, it is important to maintain positive emotions in the workplace as negative emotions can cause a downward spiral.

One developing area of research examines emotional labor, or how employees manage their emotions in the workplace to align with social norms. **Surface acting** occurs when employees outwardly display emotions that they do not feel. **Deep acting** occurs when employees actually work to change how they feel so that the emotions they are displaying are also felt. Research suggests that displaying emotions that are incongruent with how one feels can increase work stress.

Learning Processes

Understanding the basics of the learning process benefits managers, because not all employees will learn information or skills in the same manner. **Learning** is an active and purposeful process that occurs through experiences and results in permanent behavior changes. Numerous factors influence an individual's learning process, especially in an employment setting, including interest, motivation, experience, memory, ability, context, environment, perception, and maturity.

Psychological studies have led to the following three basic learning models.

Models of Learning

Classical conditioning	A behaviorist model associated with Ivan Pavlov's well-known experiment. Pavlov triggered a dog's salivary response after an association was made between the smell of food and a ringing bell.
Operant conditioning	A behaviorist model made famous by B.F. Skinner, who linked behavior with consequences. This model asserts that the consequences of actions shape voluntary behavior.
Observational learning	A social learning theory commonly associated with Albert Bandura's Bobo Doll Experiment. The model asserts that people learn by imitating behaviors observed in other people without the need for direct reinforcement. Observational learning requires attention, motor skills, motivation, and memory.

Reinforcement theory, which stems from B.F. Skinner's work, asserts that consequences influence behavior. In an organization, reinforcement theory is implemented by rewarding desirable employee behavior and punishing unwanted behavior. In psychological terms, a **reinforcer**, which can be either positive or negative, is anything that increases the probability of a specific response. The following provides a description of the four types of reinforcers and work-related examples.

Reinforcement Methods

Type of Reinforcer	Description	Example
Positive reinforcement	Providing a positive response for a desired behavior	Providing a salesperson with a bonus for exceeding a sales quota
Negative reinforcement	Withholding a negative consequence to increase a desired behavior	Eliminating an undesirable area from a salesperson's territory after the salesperson increases sales in other areas
Punishment	Giving an undesirable consequence to decrease a behavior	Suspending a salesperson for breaking a company policy
Extinction	Removing a reward to decrease a behavior	Eliminating praise for an employee's good work, which may unintentionally lower the desirable behavior

In addition to understanding the different types of reinforcers, effective managers should also understand the schedule of reinforcement. Reinforcers can either be implemented on a continuous schedule or an intermittent schedule. A manager who gives an employee a raise after every successful project is following a continuous schedule.

Continuous schedules are either on a *fixed ratio* or a *fixed interval*. A fixed ratio schedule applies reinforcement after a specific number of behavioral occurrences, whereas a fixed interval schedule applies a reinforcer after a set amount of time.

Intermittent schedules are ones that don't reinforce every instance of desired behavior and are either a *variable ratio* or a *variable interval*. Variable ratio schedules apply reinforcers after a variable number of responses, such as giving an employee a bonus after a varying number of desired behaviors occur. Variable interval schedules apply reinforcers after varying periods of time.

According to research, continuous reinforcement is the most effective way to change employee behaviors, but the method is not practical in an organization because not every behavior is observed. Therefore, intermittent schedules are more common in businesses.

Motivation

Surveys have found that most US workers are not enthusiastic about their jobs, so motivation is a serious concern for organizations. **Motivation** refers to the processes guiding an individual's intensity level, focus, and persistence. Businesses benefit from motivated employees who work hard to accomplish organizational goals, so motivation is a heavily studied topic in the field of organizational behavior. The following table summarizes the most common theories of motivation.

Motivation Theories

Maslow's Hierarchy of Needs Theory	Every individual has a hierarchy of five needs: 1. Physiological 2. Safety 3. Social 4. Esteem 5. Self-actualization The higher-order needs of social, esteem, and self-actualization are satisfied internally; the lower-order needs of physiological and safety are satisfied externally, such as through salary and tenure.
Herzberg's Two-Factor Theory	Two components on separate continuums motivate employees. Hygiene factors, such as company policies, supervision, work conditions, and salaries, lead to dissatisfaction. Motivators, such as recognition, responsibility, achievement, and advancement, lead to satisfaction.
Alderfer's ERG Theory	Individuals have three needs: 1. Existence 2. Relatedness 3. Growth Safety and physical comfort are the lowest level of existence needs. Relatedness needs involve a sense of identity in society. Growth needs are the highest level, where individuals feel a sense of accomplishment and fulfillment.
McClelland's Theory of Needs	Employee motivation is influenced by the need for achievement, power, and affiliation.
Goal-Setting Theory	Specific and challenging goals combined with feedback lead to higher levels of employee productivity.
Equity Theory	Employees derive motivation and job satisfaction by comparing their inputs, such as effort, and outcomes, such as income, with those of others. Employees then respond to eliminate any inequities.
Victor Vroom's Expectancy Theory	Employees are motivated to work hard when they believe their efforts will result in desirable outcomes, such as a good performance appraisal leading to a salary increase.

The motivation theories described in the table vary in their validity and usefulness. The **needs theories** of Maslow, Herzberg, Alderfer, and McClelland aren't generally considered valid tools for explaining employee motivation, although some research indicates a connection between achievement and productivity associated with McClelland's theory. Research into **goal-setting theory** indicates that employees are motivated by specific and difficult goals, especially when they receive feedback on their progress. However, goal-setting theory does not address issues of absenteeism, turnover, or job satisfaction. In **equity theory**, some workers are sensitive to pay inequities while others are tolerant, so it does not provide consistently accurate predictions. **Expectancy theory** is one of the most supported explanations of employee motivation because of the strong connection between effort, performance, and reward.

Job design is another managerial tool for motivating employees. Studies in job design indicate that how the elements of a job are organized can increase or decrease employee efforts. Job rotation and job enrichment are the two primary methods of redesigning a job. **Job rotation** involves periodically shifting a worker from one task to another, a technique that reduces boredom in highly routine jobs. **Job enrichment** increases an employee's responsibility and provides variety through vertical job expansion. For example, instead of having an assembly worker perform one task in the manufacturing process, the worker could assemble an entire unit.

Alternative work arrangements are another tool for motivating employees. Flextime, job sharing, and telecommuting are popular options among firms. **Flextime** offers flexible work hours for employees, such as 6:00 a.m. until 3:00 p.m. instead of the typical 8:00 a.m. to 5:00 p.m. **Job sharing** splits one 40-hour job between two or more individuals, which is a popular option for working mothers and retirees. **Telecommuting**, or working from home at least part of the week, is increasingly popular, especially for employees who spend the bulk of their workday on the computer or the phone.

An increasing number of firms are implementing reward systems through variable-pay programs to motivate workers. The following list describes the different types of variable-pay programs.
- **Piece-rate pay:** Workers receive a fixed sum for each unit produced.
- **Merit-based pay:** Compensation is based on performance appraisal ratings.
- **Bonuses:** Employees are rewarded for recent rather than historical performance.

- **Skill-based pay:** Pay levels are based on the number of skills an employee has or the number of jobs an employee can perform.
- **Profit-sharing plan:** An organization-wide plan, rather than an individual pay plan, which distributes cash or stock options based on a firm's profitability.
- **Gainsharing plan:** A group incentive plan that distributes money based on improvements in group productivity.
- **Employee stock ownership plan:** A benefits plan that lets employees obtain company stock.

Research indicates that variable-pay programs are effective tools for motivating employees and improving productivity levels. Profit-sharing plans are linked to higher levels of profitability, while gainsharing plans typically improve both worker productivity and attitude. Piece-rate plans have also been found to increase employee productivity.

Motivation theories have a number of implications for managers. Effective managers are sensitive to the individual differences of employees, so they establish individual goals, rewards, and punishments. Allowing employees to participate in setting work goals and solving productivity problems is more likely to generate motivation than dictating goals and solutions. In addition, rewards should be linked to performance, and workers should clearly understand the connection. A weak relationship between rewards and performance leads to job dissatisfaction, turnover, and absenteeism.

Work Stress

Stress occurs when an individual faces a real or perceived mental, physical, or social demand associated with an important and uncertain outcome. Work stress is an important area of study because it is estimated that approximately one third of people feel that work is very stressful. Although stress typically has negative connotations, in certain situations it can be a positive condition that increases performance levels. There are two types of stressors associated with employment: challenge stressors and hindrance stressors. **Challenge stressors** are linked to workload, deadlines, and pressure to complete tasks. **Hindrance stressors,** such as bureaucracy and office politics, prevent individuals from reaching their goal.

The primary causes of stress can be divided into three categories: environmental factors, organizational factors, and personal factors. **Environmental factors** include economic uncertainty and changes in technology. Task and role demands are examples of **organizational factors**, whereas family problems are **personal factors** influencing stress. Individuals handle stress differently based on their perceptions, job experience, and social support network. Work stress can result in short-term consequences, such as a disturbed mood, that can then turn into long-term issues, such as lost workdays. Common consequences of work stress include headaches, high blood pressure, anxiety, depression, decreased job satisfaction, absenteeism, and lower productivity.

So how can employees and organizations minimize work stress? Individuals can exercise regularly, manage their time more effectively, and talk to friends, family, and coworkers about their problems. Organization-wide strategies to reduce employee stress include improved job placement methods, effective training programs, realistic goal setting, improved communication systems, and corporate wellness programs.

INTERPERSONAL AND GROUP PROCESSES

Given that working with other people is an essential and frequent activity for managers, understanding both interpersonal and group processes is beneficial. The following section addresses group dynamics, group behavior, leadership, power, politics, and the communication process.

NOTE: Questions about interpersonal and group processes will make up 30 percent of your exam.

Group Dynamics

A **group** consists of at least two individuals who interact to achieve certain objectives. Security, status, self-esteem, affiliation, power, and goal achievement are common reasons that people join groups. Groups are designated as formal or informal.

- **Formal groups** are designated by an organization to complete specific tasks or projects, such as a sales team.
- **Informal groups** develop naturally in the workplace for the purpose of social interaction, such as workers from different departments who gather for lunch regularly.

In addition to being designated as formal or informal, groups can be classified as command, task, interest, or friendship groups. Both command and task groups are formal, while interest and friendship groups are informal. Members of a command group report to the same manager. Each member of a task group plays a different role in completing a specific task for the organization. Interest groups develop when workers share a common concern, such as improving worker safety. Friendship groups are social alliances that form at work and often continue outside of the workplace.

Groups typically develop in the same manner. The following table describes each stage of the group development process.

Group Development Stages	
Stage 1: Forming	Uncertainty among members about acceptable behaviors and group structure. Stage is complete when members feel a part of the group.
Stage 2: Storming	Characterized by intragroup conflict regarding constraints on individuality and group leadership. Stage ends with clarified hierarchy.
Stage 3: Norming	Members form close relationships and develop common expectations of member behavior.
Stage 4: Performing	Working to achieve a specific task. This is the final stage for permanent work groups.
Stage 5: Adjourning	Preparing to disband and complete tasks if group is temporary.

Just as most groups form in the same manner, groups also have common characteristics that influence member behaviors. Roles, norms, status, size, and cohesiveness are the key properties found in groups. Group members have specific roles or expected behavior patterns based on their position in a group. For example, a manager is expected to provide leadership, whereas an employee is expected to follow directions. **Norms** are the acceptable behavior standards shared by group members. Performance norms indicate how hard group members should work, while appearance norms provide cues about appropriate work attire. **Status** refers to a group member's rank and is primarily determined by power, degree of contribution, and personal characteristics.

Group performance is significantly influenced by the group's size. Research indicates that smaller groups complete tasks more quickly than larger groups and that employees work more effectively in smaller groups. **Cohesiveness** refers to how well members work together and how motivated they are to remain in the group. Because cohesiveness influences productivity, managers should strive to form smaller group, encourage goal agreement, stimulate competition with other groups, and provide rewards to the group rather than to individual members.

Group Behavior and Conflict

No matter how cohesive and productive a group or an organization is, conflicts are bound to occur. Over the years, the attitudes about workplace conflicts have changed. During the 1930s and 1940s, advocates of the traditional view of conflict asserted that conflict must be avoided because it is harmful. However, conflict can't always be avoided, which led to the interactionist view of conflict.

The interactionist school views conflict as a positive activity (in some cases) that should be encouraged to improve group performance. The interactionist view realizes that not all conflicts are beneficial, and it separates conflict into two main categories: functional and dysfunctional. **Functional conflicts** benefit group goals, whereas **dysfunctional conflicts** obstruct group performance. Functional and dysfunctional conflicts are distinguished by the following conflict types:

- **Task:** Task conflicts are associated with work goals.
- **Process:** Process conflicts stem from how work is accomplished. Low degrees of task and process conflicts can be productive if they stimulate new ideas and solutions.
- **Relationship:** Relationship conflicts stem from personality clashes between group members, and such conflicts are nearly always dysfunctional.

Conflicts typically follow a five-stage process as indicated in the following table.

Five Stages of Conflicts

Stage 1: Potential opposition or incompatibility	Conditions create opportunities for conflicts to occur. Conditions include: • Communication problems • Task structure • Personal variables
Stage 2: Cognition and personalization	Conflict issues are defined, and parties determine what a conflict is about. Emotions play a role in shaping conflict perceptions.
Stage 3: Intentions	Decisions are made to act in a certain way. The main intentions for handling conflict are: • Competing • Collaborating • Avoiding • Accommodating • Compromising
Stage 4: Behavior	Conflict becomes visible through statements, actions, and reactions by both parties.
Stage 5: Outcomes	Consequences result from the actions and reactions.

The fourth stage of the conflict process is where conflict management occurs. **Conflict management** involves using resolution and stimulation methods to manage conflict levels. Conflict-resolution methods include problem-solving sessions, expanding resources, compromising, and/or withdrawing from the conflict. Conflict-stimulation methods include realigning work groups and changing rules.

Leadership and Influences

All groups require a leader to create plans, inspire members, establish organizational structures, and achieve goals and visions. Firms benefit from understanding what makes a good leader because such knowledge improves individual, group, and organizational performance. The following table provides an overview of the various models of leadership that have been developed to identify leadership skills:

Models of Leadership	
Trait Theories	Personal qualities and characteristics of leaders differ from those of nonleaders.
Behavioral Theories	Behaviors of effective leaders differ from behaviors of ineffective leaders.
Contingency Theories	Situational variables determine whether specific leader traits and behaviors are effective or not according to the Fiedler contingency model.
Leader-Member Exchange Theory (LMX)	Leaders develop personal relationships with some members of a group, but not others. In-group subordinates exhibit better performance and job satisfaction.
Charismatic Leadership Theory	Effective leaders inspire subordinates by articulating a vision, taking risks, and perceiving the needs of others.
Transformational Leadership Theory	Leaders inspire followers by providing vision, communicating high expectations, solving problems, and giving personal attention.

Although early trait theory studies failed to isolate specific leadership traits, later research was more successful when traits were categorized alongside the Big Five personality framework. Extraversion, conscientiousness, and openness to experience are traits that have been strongly linked to effective leadership.

Behavioral theories, which suggest that leaders can be developed, focus primarily on two aspects of leadership: initiating structure and consideration. **Initiating structure** refers to the extent that leaders define their roles and the roles of employees. For example, a leader with a high degree of initiating structure assigns subordinates to specific tasks and stresses the importance of deadlines. **Consideration** relates to job relationships and the extent to which a leader helps group members, treats subordinates fairly, and shows appreciation. Studies indicate that leaders with high consideration receive more respect, and leaders with high levels of initiating structure experience high levels of group productivity.

Studies show that aspects of the Fiedler contingency model are valid. The **Fiedler model** includes eight categories, but only three categories are supported by evidence. Critics of the contingency model find the questionnaire and variables confusing and participants' scores unreliable. The Fiedler model is the most well-known contingency theory, but others include the situational leadership theory, path-goal theory, and leader-participation theory.

- **Situational leadership theory** asserts that the best action of a leader depends on the degree that followers are willing and able to complete a task.
- **Path-goal theory** asserts that it is the job of the leader to help followers accomplish goals by providing the necessary information, support, and resources. Leadership style is determined by subordinate preference and task structure.
- **Leader-participation theory** asserts that the way in which leaders make decisions is equally important to the decision itself. The decision tree for this model includes a set of twelve contingency variables, eight problem types, and five leadership styles, which can be too cumbersome for real-world managers.

The leader-member exchange theory is relatively supported by research. Studies show that leaders and followers are clearly different, with differences that are not random. Research also verifies that in-group members perform better and experience greater job satisfaction than out-group members, which is not necessarily surprising. Studies have also shown that the relationship between leaders and followers is even stronger when employees have higher levels of autonomy and control over their job performance.

Many experts believe that charismatic and transformational leadership styles are virtually the same or have only minor differences. In most cases, charismatic and transformational leadership theories are supported with evidence. Such leaders are more effective in some situations and settings than others. Charismatic or transformational leaders are most effective when interacting closely with employees, so such leaders may be more effective in small firms rather than large organizations.

While the extensive amount of leadership research may be overwhelming, managers can take the most relevant information and apply it in a business setting. The following list provides an overview of leadership implications for managers:

- Traits such as extraversion, conscientiousness, and openness to experience are typically associated with strong leaders.
- Consider the situation before assigning a leader as some leaders are task-oriented and others are people-oriented.
- Leaders who show they believe in group members by investing time and resources will most likely be rewarded with productive and satisfied employees.
- Leaders with vision, charisma, and clear communication skills are the most effective.
- Effective leaders develop relationships with group members and show that they can be trusted.

Power and Politics

Power refers to the ability that one person has to influence the behavior of another person, and in organizations, power and politics are natural and unavoidable. Effective managers understand how power functions in an organization. Power is either personal or formal. **Personal power** stems from the characteristics of an individual. The two sources of personal power are expertise and the respect of others, or referent power. **Formal power** comes from an individual's position in an organization. Sources of formal power are the ability to coerce, the ability to reward, and the formal authority to control. The following table provides an overview of the different sources of power:

Sources of Power		
Source	**Type**	**Description**
Expert power	Personal	Based on expertise, special skills, or knowledge. Physicians, tax accountants, economists, and computer specialists have power due to their expertise.
Referent power	Personal	Based on identification with an individual who possesses desirable resources or traits, such as charisma, beauty, and likability. Individuals who are admired have power over those who want to be like them. Celebrities have referent power, which is why they are commonly used to endorse products.

Sources of Power

Source	Type	Description
Coercive power	Formal	Based on an individual's fear of negative consequences for failing to obey. In the workplace, an individual who wields coercive power may have the ability to suspend, dismiss, or demote an employee. More subtle forms of coercive power involve embarrassing an individual or withholding valuable data or information.
Reward power	Formal	Based on an individual's ability to bestow valuable rewards or benefits, such as bonuses, raises, promotions, work assignments, sales territories, and work shifts.
Legitimate power	Formal	Based on an individual's position in an organization's hierarchy. Considered the most common source of power in the workplace, given its broad scope. Individuals comply with those who hold a higher rank in an organization.

Research indicates that personal sources of power are more effective than formal sources of power. Managers who exhibit expert and referent power are more likely to have satisfied employees who are committed to an organization. Coercive power has been shown to have the opposite effect. Employees are dissatisfied with their jobs and lack commitment if their manager uses negative consequences as a control method.

Although political behavior is not a formal job requirement, office politics is a reality that cannot be avoided in most organizations. Individuals with effective political skills are able to use their power sources to influence outcomes in the workplace. Within organizations, political behavior is either legitimate or illegitimate. **Legitimate actions** involve complaining to a supervisor, developing business contacts through networking, and bypassing the chain of command. **Illegitimate actions** exceed normal organizational behavior by violating implied rules of business conduct. Sabotage and whistleblowing are examples of illegitimate political behavior. Most organizational political behavior is categorized as legitimate.

According to researchers, a number of factors, both individual and organizational, determine the political environment in an organization. The following factors characterize individuals who are more likely to engage in political behaviors:

- Expect to succeed
- Perceive job alternatives because of skills, reputation, or job market
- Believe they can control their environment
- Show sensitivity to social cues and conformity
- Exhibit Machiavellian personality (manipulative and power hungry)

Organizational factors play an even greater role than individual factors in the degree to which political behaviors occur. Some organizational cultures foster politicking more than others, especially if a firm is experiencing financial difficulties or significant changes. An organizational culture characterized by minimal trust, unclear roles, and ambiguous performance evaluation systems will typically experience a high degree of political activity. A culture with low levels of trust has a higher level of political behavior and a greater likelihood of experiencing illegitimate political behavior. The following list includes the organizational factors that influence political behavior:

- Low trust
- Unclear employee roles
- Subjective performance appraisal systems
- Pressures for high performance
- Political senior managers

For many people, organizational politics are a negative aspect of the job, especially if they don't understand the dynamics of political behavior. Employees who are threatened by organizational politics experience decreased job satisfaction, increased stress, increased turnover rates, and lower performance ratings. However, politically astute individuals are more likely to view politics as an opportunity, and they are more likely to receive higher performance evaluations, more raises, and better promotions than those lacking political skills.

Communication Processes

Clear communication, defined as the transfer and understanding of meaning, is an essential element to organizational success and serves four key functions:

1. Controlling behavior
2. Fostering motivation
3. Expressing emotion
4. Providing information

Communication is a process that requires a message, a sender, and a receiver.

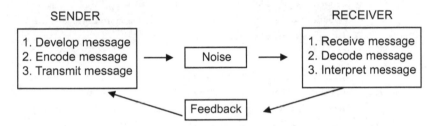

Senders initiate messages by encoding an idea through speaking, writing, gesturing, or making a facial expression. The message passes through a channel determined by the sender. Formal channels are established by an organization to transmit messages and usually follow a chain of command, while informal channels occur spontaneously. The message is directed at the receiver who must decode and interpret the message.

Communication barriers in the form of noise stand between the sender and receiver and can distort message clarity. Comprehension difficulties, cultural differences, and information overload are common noise problems. The feedback loop is the final aspect of the communication process. Feedback serves to determine whether the receiver understood the message. Group members in an organization use oral, written, and nonverbal communication to transfer meaning.

Interpersonal Communication Methods	
Oral	The vast majority of organizational communication occurs orally through such activities as speeches, one-on-one conversations, and group discussions. Quickness and immediate feedback are the advantages. Message distortions may occur if a message passes between multiple people.
Written	Memos, letters, emails, instant messages, and newsletters are used by organizations to convey written messages. Written communication provides both parties with a record of the message for future reference. Typically, written communication is more logical and clear because the sender is required to consider the message in advance. Disadvantages include the time-consuming nature of written communication and the lack of immediate feedback.
Nonverbal	Oral messages include nonverbal messages, such as body movement, tone of voice, facial expression, and physical distance between sender and receiver. Such communications provide additional meaning to a message.

Nonverbal communication involves various activities, and each one conveys a different meaning. Body language expresses how much individuals like each other and the status between the sender and receiver. For example, a sender and receiver that like and respect each other are more likely to stand close to each other. Senders that feel their status is higher than the receiver's may appear more casual, or if they feel their status is lower, they may act more formal to show deference. The most appropriate physical distance between sender and receiver often depends on cultural norms.

In addition to understanding aspects of interpersonal communication, managers should be aware that communication networks, both formal and informal, exist within organizations. The following are three primary types of formal small-group networks:

1. **Chain networks** follow a formal chain of command and are characterized by high accuracy, moderate speed, and member satisfaction.
2. **Wheel networks** depend on a central individual or leader to convey information and are characterized by high accuracy and speed but low member satisfaction.
3. **All-channel networks** allow all members to participate in communication with no single individual taking a leadership position. These networks

are characterized by high speed, high member satisfaction, and moderate accuracy.

The **grapevine** is an informal communication network that involves word-of-mouth message conveyance. Research indicates that nearly 75 percent of all employees in a firm first learn about information through the grapevine. Studies also show that approximately 75 percent of the information flowing through a grapevine is accurate. Organizational grapevines typically have the following three key characteristics:

1. Management does not control communications in the grapevine.
2. Most employees find grapevine messages more believable than messages conveyed by upper management.
3. Grapevines benefit those within the network.

Although managers cannot eliminate rumors that spread through the grapevine, they can reduce negative consequences by providing information to employees, explaining decisions, and maintaining open communication channels.

Effective communication is often distorted in an organization by a variety of barriers. The following table provides an overview of a few communication barriers.

Communication Barriers	
Filtering	Sender manipulates information so the receiver will view it more positively. For example, a sender can tell someone what they want to hear rather than the truth.
Selective perception	This is the tendency to process messages based on personal interests, experiences, and attitudes.
Information overload	Receivers select, ignore, or forget information when individuals receive more messages than they can process.
Emotions	Receivers experiencing extreme emotions, such as anger or excitement, may not interpret messages objectively.
Language	Word meanings can vary depending on the context of the communication and the experiences of the sender and receiver. Lack of language uniformity can hinder communication.

Communication Barriers	
Silence	Withholding communication is a common problem in organizations. Employees fail to report operational problems, misconduct, and harassment, which prevent management from correcting problems.
Communication apprehension	Tension and social anxiety about communicating orally and/or in writing affects 5 to 20 percent of individuals.
Gender differences	Men and women often communicate differently and for different purposes. Many men communicate to establish status and power, whereas many women communicate to provide support and connections.
Politically correct communication	Concerns about being inoffensive can prevent meaningful and accurate communication.
Politically correct communication	Word meanings can vary depending on the context of the communication and the experiences of the sender and receiver. Lack of language uniformity can hinder communication.

ORGANIZATIONAL PROCESSES AND CHARACTERISTICS

As with individuals and groups, organizations have unique processes and characteristics. The following section discusses decision-making, organizational structure, and organizational design.

....

NOTE: You will find that 15 percent of the questions you see on test day will cover organizational processes and characteristics.

....

Organizational Decision-Making

When faced with two or more alternatives, organizations, groups, and individuals must make decisions. Building new facilities, expanding services, and downsizing are examples of decisions faced by organizations. Making a decision involves interpreting information and evaluating the strengths and weaknesses of the various alternatives, which can be accomplished through the following three methods:

1. Rational decision-making
2. Bounded rationality
3. Intuitive decision-making

The **rational decision-making model** assumes that decision makers have all the available information, can identify the relevant options, and can choose the most logical and sensible option. The model involves the following six steps:

1. Define the problem.
2. Identify the decision criteria.
3. Allocate weights to the criteria.
4. Develop the alternatives.
5. Evaluate the alternatives.
6. Select the best alternative.

The rational decision-making model may involve too many assumptions that aren't viable in the real world. **Bounded rationality** accounts for some of these realities. Economist Herbert Simon first presented the theory of bounded rationality in 1982. According to Simon, individuals are faced with the following three inescapable limitations when making decisions:

1. Limited information about possible alternatives is available.
2. Individuals have a limited capacity to evaluate available information.
3. A limited amount of time is available for making decisions.

As a result, most decision makers search for solutions that are *sufficient* rather than ideal.

Making a decision based on a hunch exemplifies the **intuitive decision-making model**. Intuitive decisions occur quickly and typically rely on emotion and experience rather than quantifiable evidence. Current studies suggest that intuition can enhance rational decision-making, but it should not necessarily replace rational evaluations, especially on an organization-wide level where numerous intuitive perspectives would be unlikely to agree.

Within organizations, decisions are made by both individuals and groups. Managers benefit from knowing when it is more or less advantageous to have a decision made by a group or an individual. Groups offer a diversity of viewpoints, knowledge, and creativity that benefits the decision-making process. Moreover, decisions made by a group are more likely to be accepted and implemented by group members. However, group decision-making is a time-consuming process that involves conformity pressures, conflicts, and ambiguous responsibilities. In contrast, individuals make decisions quickly and efficiently with clear accountability for the final results.

Organizational Structure and Design

In organizations, tasks must be divided, grouped, and coordinated for the greatest efficiency, which is the purpose of having an organizational structure. **Organizational structure** involves six essential elements, as seen in the following table.

Elements of Organizational Structure	
Work specialization	The division of labor established by Henry Ford. Activities are divided into separate jobs and steps with individuals specializing in one task instead of the entire process, which can improve productivity in some industries, but decrease employee satisfaction in others.
Departmentalization	Grouping jobs to coordinate common tasks. Activities are grouped by function, product, service, geography, process, and/or customer.
Chain of command	An unbroken line of authority that reaches from the highest to the lowest levels of an organization for the purpose of clarifying authority and responsibility.
Span of control	The number of employees that a manager can effectively and efficiently oversee. This determines the number of levels and managers in an organization. A narrow span of control allows for close supervision; wider spans are more cost-effective and efficient.
Centralization/ Decentralization	The degree that decision-making is concentrated at the top of an organization's hierarchy. Top managers in centralized organizations make most decisions that are implemented by lower-level managers. Decentralized organizations assign decision-making authority to lower-level managers. Decentralization quickens problem-solving, lessens employee alienation, and allows for greater employee input.
Formalization	The extent to which jobs are governed by rules and procedures. For example, sales representatives may have more flexibility to perform their tasks than assembly-line workers who must follow specific guidelines.

Organizational design primarily consists of three classic structures; however, additional designs have been developed in recent years to account for changes in the business world. The simple structure, the bureaucracy, and the matrix structure are the most commonly implemented designs, while the virtual organization and the boundaryless organization designs are relatively new options.

Organizational Designs	
Design Type	**Characteristics**
Simple structure	• Considered a flat structure with only 2 to 3 vertical levels, minimal departmentalization, wide spans of control, centralized authority, and minimal formalization • Most commonly used in small businesses run by owner-managers who employ fewer than 50 people
Bureaucracy	• Relies on standardized work processes, specialization, highly formalized rules, centralized authority, narrow spans of control, minimal innovation, and chain-of-command decision-making
Matrix structure	• Establishes a dual chain of command • Combines functional and product departmentalization • Can cause confusion and power struggles, but can maximize activity coordination, improve the flow of information, and achieve economies of scale • Commonly used in advertising agencies, hospitals, universities, construction firms, and government agencies
Virtual organization	• Major business functions are outsourced by a small, core organization • Highly centralized with minimal, if any, departmentalization • Minimizes bureaucratic costs and long-term risks • Maximizes flexibility • Limited by unclear responsibilities, slow response time, and intermittent communication • Common in the film industry
Boundaryless organization	• Idea spurred by former GE chairman Jack Welch, who wanted to eliminate hierarchies, replace functional departments with multidisciplinary teams, and implement limitless spans of control • Used to some degree at 3M, Hewlett-Packard, and AT&T

Organization Culture and Strategy

Organizational culture consists of organizational values, ideologies, and beliefs, and how these translate to employees through socialization, practices, and organizational policies and procedures. Culture can impact the employee experience. Andrew Pettigrew introduced culture research to the field of organizational behavior in 1979 in an effort to incorporate concepts from anthropology.

Organizational culture researchers focus on things like the language, myths, stories, and history within an organization and how this impacts organizational effectiveness. In addition to these organizational artifacts leading to the development of organizational culture, leadership is also a signal of the organization's culture. For example, employees learn what the organization values by observing what leadership prioritizes and devotes resources to. Currently, there is a lack of research that demonstrates a clear linkage between organizational culture and performance. This is due to the fact that culture is difficult to study since it is hard to measure and it varies so greatly across different organizations. Researchers do agree, though, that culture can be leveraged in times of organizational change. By establishing a culture that appreciates innovation, organizational change tends to be met with less resistance.

CHANGE AND DEVELOPMENT PROCESSES

This final section addresses organizational change and organizational development, as well as the forces and processes involved with change.

NOTE: Fifteen percent of the questions on your DSST exam will cover the topics covered in this section.

Basic Processes

Given the unstable nature of economies, consumers, competitors, and markets, successful organizations must be willing to make changes when necessary. The changing workforce, technology advancements, major economic shifts, competition, social trends, and global politics pressure organizations into making changes and being flexible.

Organizations making plans to change typically turn to one of four approaches, as seen in the following table.

Processes of Change

Lewin's Three-Step Model	1. *Unfreeze:* Ensure that employees are ready for change. 2. *Change:* Implement the desired change. 3. *Refreeze:* Ensure that changes are permanent.
Kotter's Eight-Step Plan	1. Establish a sense of urgency for change. 2. Create a guiding coalition. 3. Develop a vision and strategy. 4. Convey the vision. 5. Empower and encourage others to act on the vision. 6. Plan for, create, and reward advances toward vision. 7. Reassess changes and make necessary adjustments. 8. Reinforce changes by linking them to success.

Action research	Changes based on systematically collected and analyzed data. The five steps are:
	  1. Diagnosis
	  2. Analysis
	  3. Feedback
	  4. Action
	  5. Evaluation

Organizational development	Systematic effort to improve an organization's effectiveness and adaptability by changing the attitudes, beliefs, and values of employees through long-term training programs.

Concepts of Change

Change threatens both individuals and the organization. Resistance to organizational changes can be especially harmful at a time when an organization critically needs the support and loyalty of employees. Common sources of resistance among individuals include having to change habits, worrying about security, and fearing economic changes and the unknown. In addition, individuals often process only selected information by ignoring information that challenges the security of their environment. Organization-wide resistance occurs through regulations, processes, restrictive group norms, and threats to specialized groups and power relationships.

Organizational culture plays a significant role in the change and development process. Organizations can overcome resistance by stimulating a culture of innovation, encouraging experimentation, and promoting training and development opportunities for employees. Moreover, a strong corporate culture fosters employee loyalty, which is necessary during times of major upheaval.

Applications and Techniques of Change and Development

Organizational development refers to making planned changes by improving the effectiveness of an organization through research, technology, and training. The primary values underlying organizational development methods include respecting individuals, establishing a trusting and supportive environment, de-emphasizing hierarchical control and authority, openly confronting problems, and encouraging participation in decision-making.

The following list describes organizational development methods and approaches to implementing change.

- **Sensitivity training** or **T-groups** attempt to change behavior through unstructured group interactions. Early attempts were chaotic and have been replaced by alternative methods such as **diversity training**, **executive coaching**, and **team-building exercises**, which are more structured.
- **Survey feedback** assesses attitudes and perceptions of organizational members. Data is analyzed for discrepancies, and members then gather for discussions and problem-solving.
- **Process consultation** involves hiring an outside consultant to help managers identify processes such as workflow and communication that need improvement.
- **Team building** involves interactive group activities to improve trust and communication among team members.
- **Intergroup development** attempts to alter the attitudes, stereotypes, and perceptions that group members may have towards one another. Most intergroup development sessions focus on differences between departments and occupations, such as the differences between manufacturing and financial divisions in a firm.
- **Appreciative inquiry** involves the identification of unique strengths in an organization and building on these qualities to improve performance.

The **sociotechnical** or **structural approach** to redesigning organizations focuses on meeting the needs of a changing external environment. Sociotechnical refers to the relationship between people and structure in an organization.

SUMMING IT UP

- In addition to having effective **technical skills**, managers must develop **people skills** in order to retain high-performing workers, handle employee conflicts, improve workplace productivity, and enhance both worker and firm performance. The study of **organizational behavior** provides the basis for these essential **managerial skills**.

- Early important theorists in the study of management are **Henri Fayol**, who developed the first management theory identifying five (now condensed to four) functions of managers, and **Henry Mintzberg**, who identified 10 roles of managers categorized as **interpersonal**, **informational**, and **decisional**.

- **Evidence-based management** relies on observing relationships, identifying causes and effects, and drawing conclusions based on evidence.

- **Perceptions** are how individuals organize and interpret what they experience, which may differ significantly from reality and one another's perceptions.

- Three key factors explain why employees frequently have such different perceptions: (1) the **perceiver**, (2) the **target**, and (3) the **situation**. An individual perceiver's attitudes, motives, interests, experiences, and expectations influence personal perceptions. The target or object being perceived has certain distinguishing characteristics that influence perceptions either positively or negatively.

- The methods of perceptions are **selective perception**, the **halo effect**, **contract effects**, and **stereotyping**.

- According to **attribution theory**, people try to explain the behavior of others based on internal attributes or external attributes. Behaviors because of internal attributes are under the control of an individual, whereas externally caused behaviors are out of the individual's control.

- Determining whether behavior is caused by **internal** or **external** factors depends on the factors of **distinctiveness**, **consensus**, and **consistency**.

- **The Big Five model** is supported by a large body of evidence to support the tool's five personality traits (extraversion, agreeableness, conscientiousness, emotional stability, openness to experiences) and their connection to job performance.

- **Attitudes** develop from three components: (1) cognition, (2) affect, and (3) behavior.

- Organizational behaviorists primarily focus on job satisfaction, job involvement, organizational commitment, perceived organizational support, and employee engagement.

- **Emotions** fall on two dimensions: **energy** (from low to high) and **pleasantness** (from low to high). Positive emotions tend to be associated with better outcomes for individuals and organizations. Research also shows that emotions are contagious.
- Research suggests that displaying emotions that are incongruent with how one feels can increase **work stress**.
- According to the **Rokeach Value Survey**, values can be divided into **terminal** values and **instrumental** values.
- **Learning** is an active and purposeful process that occurs through experiences and results in permanent behavior changes. The models of learning are **classical conditioning**, **operant conditioning**, and **observational conditioning**.
- **Reinforcement methods of learning** that operate in the workplace are positive reinforcement, negative reinforcement, punishment, and extinction.
- **Reinforcers** can either be implemented on a **continuous** schedule or an **intermittent** schedule.
- **Continuous schedules** are either fixed ratio or fixed interval. A **fixed ratio** schedule applies reinforcement after a specific number of behavioral occurrences, whereas a **fixed interval** schedule applies a reinforcer after a set amount of time.
- **Intermittent schedules** are ones that don't reinforce every instance of desired behavior and are either a variable ratio or a variable interval. **Variable ratio schedules** apply reinforcers after a variable number of responses. **Variable interval schedules** apply reinforcers after varying periods of time.
- The most common **motivation theories** are Maslow's hierarchy of needs, Herzberg's two-factor theory, Alderfer's ERG theory, McClelland's theory of needs, goal-setting, equity, and Victor Vroom's expectancy theory. Of these, the first four aren't considered valid for employee motivation, but the other three have some merit, especially the expectancy theory.
- **Job design** (job rotation and job enrichment) as well as alternative work arrangements (flextime, job sharing, and telecommuting) are motivational tools used by companies. Variable-pay programs (piece-rate, merit-based, bonuses, skill-based, profit-sharing, gainsharing, and employee stock ownership) are also popular ways to motivate employees.
- Two types of **stressors** are associated with employment: **challenge stressors** and **hindrance stressors**. The primary causes of stress can be divided into three categories: (1) environmental factors, (2) organizational factors, and (3) personal factors.
- Groups are **formal** or **informal**, and **command**, **task**, **interest**, or **friendship**.

- **Groups** typically develop in the same way: forming, storming, norming, performing, and adjourning, if temporary.
- Groups have common characteristics that influence member behaviors and those key properties are **roles, norms, status, size**, and **cohesiveness**. Research indicates that smaller groups complete tasks more quickly than larger groups and that employees work more effectively in smaller rather than in larger groups.
- **Interactionists** believe that, in some cases, conflict can be beneficial to the group. **Conflict** may be functional or dysfunctional. Functional and dysfunctional conflicts are distinguished by conflict type: **task, process**, and **relationship**.
- The **conflict process** has five stages: (1) potential opposition or incompatibility, (2) cognition and personalization, (3) intentions, (4) behavior, and (5) outcomes. The fourth stage is the time for conflict resolution or conflict stimulation.
- Research into **leadership styles** has produced six major models or theories that identify leadership skills: (1) **trait**, (2) **behavioral**, (3) **contingency**, (4) **leader-member exchange (LMX)**, (5) **charismatic**, and (6) **transformational**.
- **Power** in an organization is either **personal** or **formal**. The sources of personal power are expert power and referent power. The sources of formal power are coercive power, reward power, and legitimate power. Political power in an organization may be either legitimate or illegitimate.
- **Clear communication**—the transfer and understanding of meaning—is an essential element to organizational success and serves four key functions: (1) controlling behavior, (2) fostering motivation, (3) expressing emotion, and (4) providing information.
- **Communication** is a process that requires a **message**, a **sender**, and a **receiver**.
- **Barriers** to effective communication include filtering, selective perception, information overload, emotions, language, silence, communication apprehension, gender differences, and politically-correct communication.
- Making a decision involves interpreting information and evaluating the strengths and weaknesses of the various alternatives, which can be accomplished through three methods: (1) **rational decision-making**, (2) **bounded rationality**, and (3) **intuitive decision-making**.
- **Organizational structure** involves six essential elements: (1) work specialization, (2) departmentalization, (3) chain of command, (4) span of control, (5) centralization and decentralization, and (6) formalization.
- **Organizational design** may be simple, bureaucracy, matrix, virtual, or boundaryless.

- **Organizational culture** consists of an organization's values, ideologies, and beliefs and how these are translated to employees. Culture impacts employees' experiences at work and can be used to improve reactions to organizational change.
- Organizations making plans to **change** typically turn to one of four approaches: (1) Kurt Lewin's three-step model, (2) John Kotter's eight-step plan, (3) action research, and (4) organizational development.
- Common sources of **resistance** among individuals include having to change habits, worrying about security, and fearing economic changes and the unknown. Organization-wide resistance occurs through regulations, processes, restrictive group norms, and threats to specialized groups and power relationships.
- The **primary values** underlying organizational development methods include respecting individuals, establishing a trusting and supportive environment, de-emphasizing hierarchical control and authority, openly confronting problems, and encouraging participation in decision-making.

Chapter 4

Organizational Behavior Post-Test

POST-TEST ANSWER SHEET

1. Ⓐ Ⓑ Ⓒ Ⓓ	16. Ⓐ Ⓑ Ⓒ Ⓓ	31. Ⓐ Ⓑ Ⓒ Ⓓ
2. Ⓐ Ⓑ Ⓒ Ⓓ	17. Ⓐ Ⓑ Ⓒ Ⓓ	32. Ⓐ Ⓑ Ⓒ Ⓓ
3. Ⓐ Ⓑ Ⓒ Ⓓ	18. Ⓐ Ⓑ Ⓒ Ⓓ	33. Ⓐ Ⓑ Ⓒ Ⓓ
4. Ⓐ Ⓑ Ⓒ Ⓓ	19. Ⓐ Ⓑ Ⓒ Ⓓ	34. Ⓐ Ⓑ Ⓒ Ⓓ
5. Ⓐ Ⓑ Ⓒ Ⓓ	20. Ⓐ Ⓑ Ⓒ Ⓓ	35. Ⓐ Ⓑ Ⓒ Ⓓ
6. Ⓐ Ⓑ Ⓒ Ⓓ	21. Ⓐ Ⓑ Ⓒ Ⓓ	36. Ⓐ Ⓑ Ⓒ Ⓓ
7. Ⓐ Ⓑ Ⓒ Ⓓ	22. Ⓐ Ⓑ Ⓒ Ⓓ	37. Ⓐ Ⓑ Ⓒ Ⓓ
8. Ⓐ Ⓑ Ⓒ Ⓓ	23. Ⓐ Ⓑ Ⓒ Ⓓ	38. Ⓐ Ⓑ Ⓒ Ⓓ
9. Ⓐ Ⓑ Ⓒ Ⓓ	24. Ⓐ Ⓑ Ⓒ Ⓓ	39. Ⓐ Ⓑ Ⓒ Ⓓ
10. Ⓐ Ⓑ Ⓒ Ⓓ	25. Ⓐ Ⓑ Ⓒ Ⓓ	40. Ⓐ Ⓑ Ⓒ Ⓓ
11. Ⓐ Ⓑ Ⓒ Ⓓ	26. Ⓐ Ⓑ Ⓒ Ⓓ	41. Ⓐ Ⓑ Ⓒ Ⓓ
12. Ⓐ Ⓑ Ⓒ Ⓓ	27. Ⓐ Ⓑ Ⓒ Ⓓ	42. Ⓐ Ⓑ Ⓒ Ⓓ
13. Ⓐ Ⓑ Ⓒ Ⓓ	28. Ⓐ Ⓑ Ⓒ Ⓓ	43. Ⓐ Ⓑ Ⓒ Ⓓ
14. Ⓐ Ⓑ Ⓒ Ⓓ	29. Ⓐ Ⓑ Ⓒ Ⓓ	44. Ⓐ Ⓑ Ⓒ Ⓓ
15. Ⓐ Ⓑ Ⓒ Ⓓ	30. Ⓐ Ⓑ Ⓒ Ⓓ	45. Ⓐ Ⓑ Ⓒ Ⓓ

46. Ⓐ Ⓑ Ⓒ Ⓓ   51. Ⓐ Ⓑ Ⓒ Ⓓ   56. Ⓐ Ⓑ Ⓒ Ⓓ

47. Ⓐ Ⓑ Ⓒ Ⓓ   52. Ⓐ Ⓑ Ⓒ Ⓓ   57. Ⓐ Ⓑ Ⓒ Ⓓ

48. Ⓐ Ⓑ Ⓒ Ⓓ   53. Ⓐ Ⓑ Ⓒ Ⓓ   58. Ⓐ Ⓑ Ⓒ Ⓓ

49. Ⓐ Ⓑ Ⓒ Ⓓ   54. Ⓐ Ⓑ Ⓒ Ⓓ   59. Ⓐ Ⓑ Ⓒ Ⓓ

50. Ⓐ Ⓑ Ⓒ Ⓓ   55. Ⓐ Ⓑ Ⓒ Ⓓ   60. Ⓐ Ⓑ Ⓒ Ⓓ

ORGANIZATIONAL BEHAVIOR POST-TEST
72 minutes—60 questions

Directions: Carefully read each of the following 60 questions. Choose the best answer to each question and fill in the corresponding circle on the answer sheet. The Answer Key and Explanations can be found following this post-test.

1. A new employee wears expensive, stylish clothes and always looks polished. A few coworkers assume that the employee is either rich or frivolous, even though they have yet to have a conversion with this coworker. Which of the following most likely describes the perception method used by the coworkers?

   A. Selective perception
   B. Contrast effect
   C. Stereotyping
   D. Halo effect

2. Which of the following statements best summarizes goal-setting theory?

   A. Establish simple goals to improve employee job satisfaction.
   B. Address employee goals for self-identity by giving them autonomy.
   C. Set challenging goals for employees and provide them with feedback.
   D. Allow employees to set their own goals and eliminate performance appraisals.

3. The first theory of management was developed by

   A. John Kotter.
   B. Henri Fayol.
   C. Kurt Lewin.
   D. Henry Mintzberg.

4. Which of the following is NOT a commonly used research design method in the field of organizational behavior?

A. Asking a manager for their opinions
B. Case studies
C. Field experiments
D. Aggregate quantitative reviews

5. A pharmaceutical sales representative dramatically increased sales numbers in two out of three assigned sales territories. The regional manager responds by assigning the third territory, which is considered undesirable, to another sales representative, and reassigning another more desirable sales territory in its place. Which of the following methods is most likely being used by the regional manager?

A. Negative reinforcement
B. Positive reinforcement
C. Punishment
D. Extinction

6. What is the most common type of reinforcement schedule used by businesses?

A. Continuous
B. Fixed ratio
C. Intermittent
D. Fixed interval

7. Which of the following is a type of personal power?

A. Expert power
B. Reward power
C. Coercive power
D. Legitimate power

8. Which theory asserts that employees are motivated to work hard when they believe they will be rewarded?

A. ERG theory
B. Expectancy theory
C. Goal-setting theory
D. Path-goal theory

9. What is the most common source of power in the workplace?

   A. Expert power
   B. Reward power
   C. Coercive power
   D. Legitimate power

10. Which of the following is most critical to action research?

   A. Employee attitudes
   B. Organizational culture
   C. Data analysis
   D. Training

11. Which of the following is most likely to encourage a high degree of political behavior within an organization?

   A. Pressures to excel
   B. Union involvement in human resources
   C. Over-structured employee roles
   D. Objective performance appraisal systems

12. A sales manager reaches a deal with the firm's CEO to implement flexible scheduling for the sales department. The sales manager is most likely acting as a

   A. liaison.
   B. negotiator.
   C. figurehead.
   D. disseminator.

13. Members of a command group are more likely to

   A. belong to the same union.
   B. work in different departments.
   C. share the same manager.
   D. interact socially.

14. Which of the following is an example of an environmental factor that can cause work stress?

   A. Task demands
   B. Role demands
   C. Family problems
   D. Changes in technology

15. According to the path-goal theory, leadership style is determined by

    A. leader characteristics.
    B. reward immediacy.
    C. group relationships.
    D. task structure.

16. According to LMX theory research, the relationship between managers and employees grows stronger when

    A. employees have greater autonomy.
    B. managers are open to new experiences.
    C. employees are assigned challenging tasks.
    D. managers have charisma and long-term vision.

17. What is an advantage of oral communication?

    A. Expresses emotions clearly
    B. Provides immediate feedback
    C. Minimizes common noise problems
    D. Allows for logical message formation

18. Group hierarchy is most likely established during which stage of group development?

    A. Norming
    B. Forming
    C. Storming
    D. Performing

19. Which of the following is NOT a benefit of group decision-making over individual decision-making?

    A. Diversity of viewpoints
    B. Quicker decisions
    C. Diversity of knowledge
    D. Higher degree of acceptance by others

20. What is the primary criticism of the Fiedler model?

    A. Vague connections between leader behaviors and traits
    B. Confusion regarding the questionnaire and variables
    C. Inadequate support from psychological assessments
    D. Failure to isolate specific leadership characteristics

21. Which of the following is NOT a field that contributes to organizational behavior?

    A. Psychology
    B. Anthropology
    C. Geology
    D. Sociology

22. Which decision-making method assumes that individuals face limitations on information and time when making decisions?

    A. Intuitive decision-making
    B. Rational decision-making
    C. Bounded rationality
    D. Work specialization

23. When employees display emotions that they are not actually feeling, this is called

    A. surface acting.
    B. the affective circumplex model.
    C. deep acting.
    D. emotional contagion.

24. Performance norms primarily indicate

    A. the way that group members should communicate.
    B. how group members are expected to behave.
    C. how hard group members should work.
    D. the roles that group members should play.

25. A firm that groups jobs by product is most likely using which element of organizational structure?

    A. Formalization
    B. Departmentalization
    C. Work specialization
    D. Centralization

26. Which of the following is the most commonly used personality assessment tool?

    A. Myers-Briggs Type Indicator
    B. Sentence completion test
    C. Thematic apperception test
    D. Big Five model

27. Which aspect of organizational structure was first established by Henry Ford?

  A. Departmentalization
  B. Span of control
  C. Work specialization
  D. Formalization

28. Which of the following is NOT a driver of employee culture?

  A. Leadership
  B. Organizational policies
  C. A competitor's products and services
  D. Myths

29. Which of the following statements best summarizes Mintzberg's study?

  A. Some management roles are more important than others.
  B. The leadership role is most directly connected to success.
  C. Most management roles are decision-oriented.
  D. All roles of management are interrelated.

30. Which of the following is a major feature of a bureaucratic organization?

  A. Dual chains of command
  B. Standardized work processes
  C. Minimal departmentalization
  D. Decentralized authority

31. Which of the following activities is LEAST likely to occur at a firm implementing an organizational development strategy?

  A. Distributing surveys to work units
  B. Hiring an outside process consultant
  C. Developing new job specifications
  D. Planning team-building activities

32. According to the interactionist view of conflict, which of the following is most likely a dysfunctional conflict?

  A. Personality clashes
  B. Different work objectives
  C. Communication breakdowns
  D. Unclear work assignment procedures

33. Which type of stressor is linked to workload, deadlines, and pressure to complete tasks?

A. Challenge stressors
B. Hindrance stressors
C. Task stressors
D. Emotional stressors

34. Which term refers to the extent to which employees care about their jobs?

A. Job satisfaction
B. Job involvement
C. Employee engagement
D. Employee commitment

35. During the cognition stage of the conflict process, which of the following statements describes what is most likely to occur?

A. Conditions create conflict opportunities.
B. Emotions shape conflict perceptions.
C. Conflicts are actively avoided.
D. Conflicts become visible.

36. From which field did organizational culture research originate from?

A. Sociology
B. Social psychology
C. Psychology
D. Anthropology

37. Which of the following involves basing managerial decisions on a systematic study of the best available research?

A. Evidence-based management
B. Analytical management
C. Strategic management
D. Rational management

38. Which of the following is NOT one of the primary values underlying organizational development methods?

A. Emphasizing hierarchical control and authority
B. Respecting individuals
C. Openly confronting problems
D. Encouraging participation in decision-making.

39. A manager is interviewing job candidates. The first three applicants are clearly unqualified for the position. The manager offers the position to the last interviewee, who lacks experience, but has a better personality for the job than the other candidates. Which of the following has most likely occurred?

A. Halo effect
B. Stereotyping
C. Contrast effect
D. Selective perception

40. Which term refers to identifying and building on an organization's unique strengths during the process of organizational change?

A. Process consultation
B. Appreciative inquiry
C. Intergroup development
D. SWOT analysis

41. For which of the following scenarios is employee loyalty particularly beneficial?

A. When employees experience stress
B. During organizational change
C. When employees are low in motivation
D. When making group decisions

42. Which of the following approaches to implementing change is described by the identification of unique strengths in an organization and building on these qualities to improve performance?

A. Sensitivity training
B. Process consultation
C. Appreciative inquiry
D. Team building

43. Which of the following is a conflict-stimulation method?

A. Realigning work groups
B. Holding problem-solving sessions
C. Developing joint compromises
D. Expanding group resources

44. All of the following factors help determine whether a person's behavior is caused by internal or external issues EXCEPT:

A. Consensus
B. Personality
C. Consistency
D. Distinctiveness

45. The transformational leadership theory is most similar to which of the following?

A. LMX theory
B. Contingency theory
C. Behavioral theory
D. Charismatic leadership theory

46. Which of the following is asserted by the interactionist school of thought?

A. Conflict can improve group performance.
B. Conflict always harms group productivity.
C. Conflict can be minimized by strong leadership.
D. Conflict benefits small groups but not large ones.

47. Which process of change is the systematic effort to improve an organization's effectiveness and adaptability by changing the attitudes, beliefs, and values of employees through long-term training programs?

A. Lewin's three-step model
B. Kotter's eight-step plan
C. Action research
D. Organizational development

48. Feeling anxious about making an oral presentation at work is an example of a/an

A. illegitimate job behavior.
B. communication barrier.
C. nonverbal cue.
D. chain network.

49. For a couple of weeks, an employee has been working longer than normal hours to complete an important project. However, the manager has not exhibited any appreciation for the extra effort, so the employee's motivation has diminished. Which type of reinforcement method has most likely been used by the manager?

A. Negative reinforcement
B. Positive reinforcement
C. Punishment
D. Extinction

50. Which of the following is NOT a key function of communication in an organization?

A. Increasing performance
B. Controlling behavior
C. Expressing emotion
D. Fostering motivation

51. According to the Big Five model, a worker with which personality trait is more likely to have a workplace accident?

A. Extraversion
B. Agreeableness
C. Emotional stability
D. Openness to experience

52. According to the bounded rationality model of decision-making, which of the following is NOT one of the limitations individuals have when making a decision?

A. Only limited information about possible alternatives is available
B. Individuals are often indecisive
C. Individuals have a limited capacity to evaluate available information
D. Only a limited amount of time is available for making decisions

53. Which of the following is most likely a true statement about groups?

A. Competition within a group is detrimental to productivity.
B. Small groups complete tasks more quickly than large groups.
C. Employers stimulate productivity by rewarding individuals rather than entire groups.
D. Employees work more productively and cohesively in large groups than in small groups.

54. Which of the following consists of an organization's values, ideologies, and beliefs and how these are translated to employees through socialization, practices, and policies?

A. Leadership style
B. Organizational design
C. Organizational structure
D. Organizational culture

55. An employee received a bonus after six months of employment The employee then received an additional bonus seven months later and another bonus twelve months later. Assuming that the bonuses don't correspond to specific accomplishments, which type of reinforcement schedule is most likely being used by the employer?

A. Continuous schedule
B. Variable interval schedule
C. Fixed ratio schedule
D. Variable ratio schedule

56. The purpose of the third step in Kurt Lewin's model is to

A. ensure that organizational change is permanent.
B. prepare employees for organizational changes.
C. implement desired organizational changes.
D. develop an organizational change plan.

57. Which of the following is NOT a way for employees and organizations to minimize work stress?

A. Using effective training programs
B. Job reassignment
C. Regular exercise
D. Realistic goal setting

58. An employee with a high degree of agreeableness is most likely to have

    A. lower levels of job performance.
    B. better negotiation skills.
    C. lower levels of career success.
    D. more detail-oriented skills.

59. What is the primary benefit of job rotation?

    A. Expanding work teams
    B. Minimizing employee boredom
    C. Appealing to working mothers
    D. Increasing an employee's responsibilities

60. Which of the following is a terminal value according to the Rokeach Value Survey?

    A. Honesty
    B. Sincerity
    C. Equality
    D. Dependability

ANSWER KEY AND EXPLANATIONS

1. D	13. C	25. B	37. A	49. D
2. C	14. D	26. A	38. A	50. A
3. B	15. D	27. C	39. C	51. D
4. A	16. A	28. C	40. B	52. B
5. A	17. B	29. D	41. B	53. B
6. C	18. C	30. B	42. C	54. D
7. A	19. B	31. C	43. A	55. B
8. B	20. B	32. A	44. B	56. A
9. D	21. C	33. A	45. D	57. B
10. C	22. C	34. B	46. A	58. C
11. A	23. A	35. B	47. D	59. B
12. B	24. C	36. D	48. B	60. C

1. **The correct answer is D.** Drawing general impressions of a person based on one characteristic, such as appearance, suggests the halo effect. Selective perception (choice A) occurs when people interpret select observations of another person based on personal interests, experiences, and attitudes. Contrast effect (choice B) involves making comparisons. Stereotyping (choice C) is judging based on group association, such as an ethnic group.

2. **The correct answer is C.** Research related to goal-setting theory indicates that employees are motivated by specific and difficult goals, especially when they receive feedback on their progress. Choice A is incorrect because goals should be challenging, not simple. Choices B and D are not relevant to goal-setting theory.

3. **The correct answer is B.** Fayol established the first theory of management. John Kotter (choice A) and Kurt Lewin (choice C) developed organizational change theories. Henry Mintzberg (choice D) followed Fayol by identifying ten roles of managers.

4. **The correct answer is A.** Asking managers for their opinions is not a systematic method of study. Research design methods that are commonly used in organizational behavior research are case studies (choice B), field surveys, laboratory experiments, field experiments (choice C), and aggregate quantitative reviews (choice D).

5. **The correct answer is A.** Negative reinforcement involves withholding a negative consequence to increase a desired behavior. In this case, the undesirable territory was assigned to another sales representative because of the dramatic increase in sales. A bonus is a type of positive reinforcement (choice B). A suspension is an example of punishment (choice C). Extinction (choice D) removes a reward to decrease behavior.

6. **The correct answer is C.** Intermittent schedules are the most common type of reinforcement schedule used by businesses. Continuous reinforcement (choice A) is the most effective way to change employee behaviors, but it is impractical. Fixed ratio (choice B) and fixed interval (choice D) are types of continuous reinforcement.

7. **The correct answer is A.** Expert power is a personal power that is based on an individual's expertise or knowledge. Reward power (choice B), coercive power (choice C), and legitimate power (choice D) are formal powers that stem from an individual's position in an organization.

8. **The correct answer is B.** Expectancy theory is one of the most supported explanations of employee motivation because of the strong connection between effort, performance, and reward. ERG theory (choice A) asserts that individuals need existence, relatedness, and growth. Goal-setting theory (choice C) doesn't link effort with rewards. Path-goal theory (choice D) is a leadership theory.

9. **The correct answer is D.** Legitimate power stems from an individual's position in a firm and is the most common source of power in the workplace because of its broad scope. Expert power (choice A), reward power (choice B), and coercive power (choice C) are less common in work environments.

10. **The correct answer is C.** With action research, organizational changes are based on systematically collected and analyzed data. Employee attitudes (choice A), organizational culture (choice B), and training (choice D) are less relevant.

11. **The correct answer is A.** A culture that pressures employees to excel is more likely to foster political behaviors. Union involvement in human resources (choice B) is irrelevant. It is unlikely that over-structured employee roles (choice C) and objective performance appraisal systems would foster a high degree of political behavior. In fact, the opposite would be true. Unclear employee roles and subjective performance appraisal systems are more likely to encourage political behavior among workers.

12. **The correct answer is B.** The negotiator role involves bargaining with others to obtain advantages. The liaison (choice A) and figurehead (choice C) are both interpersonal roles that involve developing and maintaining good relationships with people. The disseminator role (choice D) relates to providing information to subordinates.

13. **The correct answer is C.** Members of a command group report to the same manager. Choice A is not the best answer because command group members may or may not belong to a union. Choice B is incorrect because task group members are more likely to work in different departments. Choice D is incorrect because friendship group members interact outside of work.

14. **The correct answer is D.** Changes in technology are considered to be external to the individual and the organization, driven by innovations in society. Task demands (choice A) and role demands (choice B) are organizational factors. Family problems (choice C) are categorized as personal factors.

15. **The correct answer is D.** Leadership style is determined by subordinate preference and task structure, according to the path-goal theory. Leader characteristics (choice A), personal rewards (choice B), and group relationships (choice C) are not relevant to path-goal theory.

16. **The correct answer is A.** Leader-member exchange studies have shown that the relationship between leaders and followers is even stronger when employees have higher levels of autonomy and control over their job performance. Leaders who are open to new experiences (choice B) are typically strong, but this is not linked to LMX theory. Choices C and D aren't necessarily associated with LMX theory.

17. **The correct answer is B.** Immediate feedback and speed are the main advantages of oral communication. Emotions (choice A) are not necessarily expressed clearly through oral communication. Noise problems (choice C) remain with oral communication. Written communication (choice D) is typically more logical because people have time to consider what they want to communicate.

18. **The correct answer is C.** The storming stage is characterized by intragroup conflict regarding group leadership, and it ends with a clarified hierarchy. Hierarchy is typically not established during the norming (choice A), forming (choice B), or performing (choice D) stages of group development.

19. **The correct answer is B.** Individual decisions take less time than group decisions. Group decision-making is advantageous because it incorporates more viewpoints (choice A), members typically have diversity in their knowledge (choice C), and there tends to be a higher degree of acceptance for group decisions (choice D).

20. **The correct answer is B.** Critics of the Fiedler model find the questionnaire and variables confusing and participants' scores unreliable. Choices A, C, and D are criticisms, but not necessarily associated with Fiedler's contingency theory.

21. **The correct answer is C.** Geology is not a field that contributes to organizational behavior. Psychology (choice A), anthropology (choice B), and sociology (choice D) all contribute to organizational behavior.

22. The correct answer is C. Bounded rationality assumes that individuals face limitations when making decisions: limited information, limited capacity, and limited time. Intuitive (choice A) and rational (choice B) decision-making models don't account for such limitations. Work specialization (choice D) is not related to the decision-making process.

23. The correct answer is A. Surface acting is where employees display emotions that they are not actually feeling. The affective circumplex model (choice B) is a way to delineate emotions according to how they fall on two dimensions: energy and pleasantness. Deep acting (choice C) occurs when individuals change the emotions they feel so that it matches the emotions they are displaying. Emotional contagion (choice D) refers to when an individual's emotion causes others to feel the same way.

24. The correct answer is C. Performance norms indicate how hard group members should work. Communication (choice A), behavior (choice B), and roles (choice D) are less likely to be indicated by performance norms.

25. The correct answer is B. Departmentalization involves grouping jobs by product, function, or geography for the purpose of coordinating tasks. Formalization (choice A) is the degree to which rules govern jobs. Work specialization (choice C) divides labor into separate jobs to improve productivity. Centralized organizations (choice D) rely on top managers to make decisions.

26. The correct answer is A. The Myers-Briggs Type Indicator (MBTI) is the most frequently used personality assessment tool.

27. The correct answer is C. The division of labor, or work specialization, was established by Henry Ford. Ford is not credited for establishing departmentalization (choice A), span of control (choice B), or formalization (choice D). Span of control originated in the military.

28. The correct answer is C. Since culture comes from within an organization, a competitors' products and services would not drive employee culture. Leadership (choice A), organizational policies and practices (choice B), and organizational myths (choice D) are all important in translating culture to employees.

29. The correct answer is D. Each management role is connected to another. Mintzberg's study doesn't suggest that some roles are more important than others (choice A) or more related to success (choice B). Choice C is incorrect because roles are equally distributed among interpersonal, information, and decisional.

30. The correct answer is B. Bureaucracies are characterized by standardization, departmentalization, and centralized authority. This eliminates choices C and D as correct. Since dual chains of command (choice A) is an element of the matrix structure and not a bureaucratic organization, this leaves choice B as the correct answer.

31. The correct answer is C. Changing job specifications is least likely to occur during the process of organizational development. A firm is more likely to distribute surveys to collect feedback about perceptions (choice A), hire an outside consultant to assess processes (choice B), and implement team building activities (choice D).

32. The correct answer is A. Relationship conflicts stem from personality clashes between group members, and such conflicts are nearly always dysfunctional.

33. The correct answer is A. Challenge stressors are linked to workload, deadlines, and pressure to complete tasks. Hindrance stressors (choice B) prevent individuals from reaching their goals, such as bureaucracy and politics. Task (choice C) and emotional stressors (choice D) are not categories.

34. **The correct answer is B.** The extent to which employees identify with and care about their jobs is termed job involvement. Job satisfaction (choice A) refers to an employee's positive or negative feelings about a job. Employee engagement (choice C) relates to enthusiasm. Employee commitment (choice D) is not an organizational behavior term.

35. **The correct answer is B.** In the cognition and personalization stage, parties determine what a conflict is about, and emotions play a role in shaping conflict perceptions.

36. **The correct answer is D.** Organizational culture research comes from anthropology. In the 1970s, anthropology researchers introduced it to the field of organizational behavior in an effort to increase the use of anthropology concepts in organizational behavior research.

37. **The correct answer is A.** Evidence-based management calls for managers to base decisions on the best available scientific evidence rather than feelings and intuitions. Analytical management (choice B) uses mathematical models to develop solutions to business problems. Strategic management (choice C) is the process for designing and implementing competitive steps to enhance the performance of an organization. Rational management (choice D) seems like a good answer, but it is not the best answer.

38. **The correct answer is A.** Organizational development actually works to de-emphasize hierarchical control and authority. Respecting individuals (choice B), openly confronting problems (choice C), and encouraging participation in decision-making (choice D) are all central to organizational development.

39. **The correct answer is C.** Contrast effect occurs when a person is evaluated based on comparisons to another person. Halo effect (choice A) involves making a general impression based on one characteristic. There is no indication that stereotyping (choice B) based on a group association has occurred. Selective perception (choice D) is a problem associated with narrow interpretations.

40. **The correct answer is B.** Appreciative inquiry involves the identification of unique strengths in an organization and building on these qualities to improve performance. Process consultation (choice A) and intergroup development (choice C) are other organizational methods. A SWOT analysis (choice D) is based on strengths, weaknesses, opportunities, and threats, and is used for marketing purposes.

41. **The correct answer is B.** Employee loyalty is particularly beneficial during organizational change. Choices A, C, and D are incorrect because there is no evidence to suggest that employee loyalty has an impact on stress, motivation, or decision-making outcomes.

42. **The correct answer is C.** Appreciative inquiry identifies unique strengths in an organization and builds on those qualities to improve performance. Sensitivity training (choice A) changes behavior using things such as diversity training and executive coaching. Process consultation (choice B) involves hiring an outside consultant to help managers identify processes that need to be improved. Team building (choice D) entails interactive group activities to improve group trust and communication.

43. **The correct answer is A.** Conflict-stimulation methods include realigning work groups and changing rules. Conflict-resolution, not conflict-stimulation, methods include problem-solving sessions (choice B), compromising (choice C), and expanding resources (choice D).

44. **The correct answer is B.** According to attribution theory, consensus (choice A), consistency (choice C), and distinctiveness (choice D) are the primary factors that determine whether a person's behavior is internally or externally caused. Personality is not a consideration.

45. The correct answer is D. Transformational leadership theory and charismatic leadership theory both suggest that leaders articulate a vision and are inspirational. LMX theory (choice A) is about the relationship between leaders and followers and indicates that the more autonomy employees have, the stronger the relationship. Contingency theory (choice B) posits that situational variables determine whether specific leadership traits and behaviors are effective. With behavioral theory (choice C), effective leaders have different behaviors compared to ineffective leaders.

46. The correct answer is A. The interactionist school of thought views conflict as a positive activity in some cases and should be encouraged in those situations in order to improve group performance.

47. The correct answer is D. Organizational development is the systematic effort to improve an organization's effectiveness and adaptability by changing the attitudes, beliefs, and values of employees through long-term training programs. Lewin's three-step model (choice A), Kotter's eight-step plan (choice B), and action research (choice C) have different approaches to changing the organization; none of them focus specifically on using training to change attitudes, beliefs, and values of employees.

48. The correct answer is B. Communication apprehension occurs when a person feels tense about communicating orally, and it is a type of communication barrier that affects nearly 20 percent of all workers.

49. The correct answer is D. Failing to show appreciation for help or failing to compliment employees for working hard are examples of extinction. Negative reinforcement (choice A) involves removing an undesirable consequence. Neither positive reinforcement (choice B) nor punishment (choice C) apply in this scenario.

50. The correct answer is A. Increased performance may result from clear communication, but it isn't a primary function. The four functions of communication in an organization are controlling behavior (choice B), expressing emotion (choice C), fostering motivation (choice D), and providing information.

51. **The correct answer is D.** Individuals who score high on openness to experience are more creative, but more susceptible to workplace accidents. Extraversion (choice A), agreeableness (choice B), and emotional stability (choice C) are not necessarily associated with risky behavior at work.

52. **The correct answer is B.** The model of bounded rationality assumes that there are three limitations when making decisions: (1) only a limited information about possible alternatives is available (choice A), (2) individuals have a limited capacity to evaluate available information (choice C), and (3) only a limited amount of time is available for making decisions (choice D). An individual's indecisiveness is not a part of the model.

53. **The correct answer is B.** Research indicates that smaller groups complete tasks more quickly than larger groups and that employees work more effectively in smaller rather than larger groups.

54. **The correct answer is D.** While leadership can influence organizational culture, it is the culture itself that translates an organization's values, ideologies, and beliefs. Organizational design (choice B) and organizational structure (choice C) refer to how the organization is configured in terms of things like power and employees.

55. **The correct answer is B.** Variable interval schedules apply reinforcers after varying periods of time. Continuous schedule (choice A) and fixed ration schedule (choice C) are incorrect because the employee didn't receive bonuses after every success. Variable ratio schedules (choice D) apply reinforcers after a variable number of responses, which isn't suggested by the information given in the question.

56. **The correct answer is A.** The purpose of the third and final step of Lewin's model is to ensure that organizational changes are permanent. Employees are prepared (choice B) and a plan is made (choice D) in the first step. Plans are implemented (choice C) in the second step.

57. **The correct answer is B.** Research has not shown that job reassignment is effective at minimizing work stress. Using effective training programs (choice A), regular exercise (choice C), and realistic goal setting (choice D) are all proven methods to decrease work stress in employees.

58. **The correct answer is C.** Agreeableness is associated with high job performance, low levels of career success, and poor negotiation skills. Based in this information, the opposite of choices A and B is true so these choices can be eliminated. Conscientiousness, not agreeableness, implies better attention to detail, making choice D incorrect.

59. **The correct answer is B.** Job rotation involves periodically shifting a worker from one task to another, a technique that reduces boredom in highly routine jobs.

60. **The correct answer is C.** According to the Rokeach Value Survey, values can be divided into two types: (1) terminal values and (2) instrumental values. Equality is a terminal value. Honesty (choice A), sincerity (choice B), and dependability (choice D) are instrumental values.

Like what you see? Get unlimited access to Peterson's full catalog of DSST practice tests, instructional videos, flashcards, and more at **www.petersons.com/testprep/dsst**.

Printed in the USA
CPSIA information can be obtained
at www.ICGtesting.com
JSHW012044140824
68134JS00033B/3248